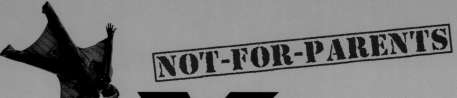

eXTREME PLANET

EXPLORING THE MOST EXTREME STUFF ON EARTH!

NOT-FOR-PARENTS

eXtreme PLANET

EXPLORING THE MOST EXTREME STUFF ON EARTH!

MICHAEL DUBOIS   KATRI HILDEN

NOT-FOR-PARENTS

EXTREME PLANET

Here at Lonely Planet we decided to make a book all about the fascinating extremes that you can experience in our amazing world. **WARNING:** there's a serious YUCK factor within these pages, so it might be best to keep this book well away from MUM and DAD...

Hang on for the ride of your life around the planet's HOTTEST, *wettest,* **deepest,** coldest, HIGHEST, **driest**, *windiest* and all-round **wildest** places.

Meet some of the most strangely different people – as well as the **biggest,** SMALLEST, *smelliest,* **slimiest,** WEIRDEST and **kookiest** critters

that share this strange and wonderful world of ours.

To begin your tour of our

EXTREME PLANET,

just turn the page...

CONTENTS

Walk this way. Millipedes are the **leggiest critters**. They have up to **400 tiny legs**, but can't walk very fast. Centipedes, their close relatives, have between 20 and 300 legs.

All mixed up. When scientists first saw an **Australian platypus**, they thought it was a make-believe animal that someone had stitched together as a prank. It has a rubbery beak like a **duck**, feet like an **otter** and a tail like a **beaver**. Along with the spiky Australian echidna, it is the **only mammal** in the world that **lays eggs**. It is also one of the world's few **venomous** mammals – the males have a poison-filled **spike** on their back feet.

ANIMALIA

Some of the biggest and best bits from the animal kingdom.

African ostriches have the most lethal legs. With their longest, strongest bird's legs they can run at **72km/h** (45mph)! And cover 3–5m (10–16ft) in a single stride. They can **kick you to death** with their long, sharp toe claws.

Can you clean your eyes and ears with your tongue? Giraffes can! They have the **longest neck** of any animal, about **1.8m** (6ft), and the **longest tail** (up to 2.4m/8ft). Why were they once called **'camel-leopards'**? Because their head looks like a **camel head**, they can go a long time without drinking water, and they have spots like a **leopard**!

WHAT ARE YOU STARING AT?

THE FACE ONLY A MOTHER COULD LOVE!

EARS: Elephants have the **world's biggest ears**. They flap them like fans, to keep themselves cool. **HORNS:** The **wild water buffalo** from Southeast Asia has the **longest horns** – up to 2m (79in) from tip to tip. **EYES: Colossal squid** have the **world's biggest eyes** – bigger than dinner plates, at about 28cm (11in). These huge deep-sea dwellers need them to see in dark water, as they can live over 2km (6500ft) deep. Bet you didn't know squid and octopus also have three hearts, and blue-green blood! **TEETH: Sharks** have the **deadliest teeth**. Not just one row, but several rows that keep growing and moving forward to replace old ones that wear out. They lose about 30,000 teeth in their lifetime. **MOUSTACHE:** The prize for the neatest, **nicest moustache** goes to the **emperor tamarin monkey**, from the Amazon.

INTO THE DEEP

Time for an underwater adventure!

Deepest ocean voyage

In 1960, an **underwater vehicle** known as a **bathyscaphe** ('deep ship') made it down as deep as people can ever go. The ship was called the **Trieste**, and in it were Swiss oceanographer **Jacques Piccard** and US Navy Lieutenant **Don Walsh**. They reached the floor of the **Mariana Trench** in the **Pacific Ocean**, 10,911m (35,797ft) below the surface. This trench is the **deepest point in the ocean**.

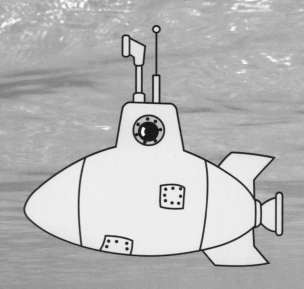

DEEP DIVERS

Human unassisted free dive
100m (328ft)

Deepest bird
565m (1854ft)

Deepest reptile
640m (2100ft)

Deepest mammal
2500m (8200ft)

Don't breathe out

Can you hold your breath for more than **100 minutes?** That's what **elephant seals** do when they dive down looking for food. The deep diving record by a seal goes to a **southern elephant seal,** spotted **2388m (7835ft)** beneath the waves.

Mariana Trench

10,911m (35,797ft)

Spring Temple Buddha   128m (420ft)
Great Pyramid of Giza   146m (480ft)
Burj Khalifa   828m (2717ft)

Mount Everest   8848m (29,029ft)

The world's biggest ocean trench, the **Mariana Trench**, is so deep that if you stacked **Mt Everest** PLUS the world's tallest building, the **Burj Khalifa** of the United Arab Emirates, PLUS the **Great Pyramid of Giza** of Egypt on top of that, PLUS the world's tallest statue, the **Spring Temple Buddha** in China, on top of that, there would still be almost **1000m (3281ft) of water above it!**

Ain't no sunshine

Back in **1977**, scientists in a **deep sea submarine** found holes in the **bottom of the ocean**, spewing out **boiling hot water** from deep within the Earth. They also found **bacteria** living here – just about the **only life on Earth** that doesn't depend on the sun. Instead, it lives on the **chemical energy** in the **boiling water**. Other **animals** then feed on the bacteria.

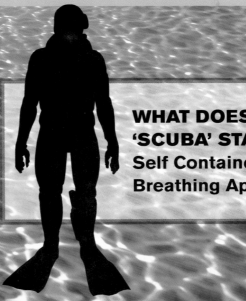

WHAT DOES THE WORD 'SCUBA' STAND FOR?
Self Contained Underwater Breathing Apparatus

6,000,000,000,000,000

That's how many **sheets of paper** you could make from the **wood in all the trees** in the Amazon.

Head shrinkers

The **Shuar** people in **Ecuador** and **Peru** used to **shrink the heads** of people they **killed**. They would take out the **skull**, **sew up the eyes and mouth,** then boil the flesh before drying it. The Shuar thought they could get hold of the **person's soul** by shrinking their head.

No TV or mobiles here

The Amazon rainforest is so huge that there are still **thousands of people living** in it who have **never had contact** with the **modern outside world**.

Gimme some air

The Amazon rainforest is nicknamed the '**lungs of the planet**'. Its billions of trees produce **20 per cent of the world's oxygen**, which we need to breathe.

I'd like to sssquash you ...

Be careful here of **anacondas**, the **world's biggest snake**. These **7.6m (25ft)** long giants can **wrap themselves around you, crush you, then gobble you whole, head first**. But it's just a baby compared to the monster snake fossil that scientists found in a coal mine in Colombia in 2008. It was **as long as a bus** and **weighed as much as a small car**. Lucky it lived **60 million years ago**!

SOUTH AMERICA

The Amazon rainforest covers more than **6.5 million sq km (2.5 million sq mi)**. That's over a **billion acres**. It is nearly as big as Australia. It covers about **half of Brazil**, as well as some of **Venezuela**, **Colombia**, **eastern Ecuador** and **Peru**. No other place on **Earth** is richer in life. More than **one-third of all species in the world live here**, including over **500 mammal**, **175 lizard** and over **300 other reptile species** ... oh, and **millions** of **insect varieties**.

JUNGLE FEVER

The Amazon rainforest is the world's biggest and most AMAZING jungle.

ROASTED OR FRIED?

Feeling peckish?

Goliath bird-eaters are the **world's largest spiders** – but that doesn't stop hungry kids making a tasty afternoon snack out of these **28cm (11in)** monsters. Kids hunt them out of their burrows, **roast them over a fire** and **munch on their legs**. They even use the spider **fangs** as toothpicks.

'He who kills in one leap'

Jaguars are the **biggest cats** in South America. They **kill** by leaping on prey from a sneaky spot. They are fine **tree** climbers and not bad **swimmers**.

Canopy capers

This incredibly vast jungle is so **thick** that **very little sunlight** reaches the forest floor, and very few plants actually live down there. **Most of the action** takes place at **the top of the trees**, called the **canopy**. Some animals **live all their lives up there** and **never come down to the ground**.

Titan beetles are enormous. Their bodies can grow up to **17cm (6.5in)** long. With such a **huge tummy**, you would think they would have a **monster** appetite to match. Curiously, the adult male titan **never eats**. It simply **flies** around looking to match up with a lady titan until it **dies**!

LIVING IN EXTREMES

Over 7 billion people live on Planet Earth, in the most surprising places …

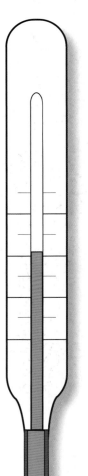

70.7°C (160°F)
Hottest land surface temperature ever recorded
Dasht-e Lut desert, Iran. You could fry an egg on this!

57.8°C (136°F)
Hottest air temperature ever recorded
Al-Aziziya, Libya. This is way too hot to go to school!

50°C (122°F)
Hottest place where people live
Imagine living in a spot where it often gets this hot and it rarely rains. The Tuareg people have adapted to living in such heat in Africa's Sahara desert. They live in tents, wear loose robes and cross the desert on camels.

−47°C (−53°F)
Coldest city in the world
If you live in Yakutsk, Siberia, you might need to wear a few pairs of underpants and lots of layers of fur and wool when you go out to play … because this is how unbelievably cold it often gets in this Russian city. It's a good place to snuggle up with a Siberian husky.

Most NORTHERN capital
Reykjavík, Iceland: 2874km
(1786mi) from North Pole

Most SOUTHERN capital
Wellington, New Zealand: 5420km
(3368mi) from South Pole

Coldest temperature WAS HERE!
Vostok Station, a Russian research station in Antarctica. The temperature fell to **−89.2°C** (−128.6°F) on 21 July 1983.
Brrr!

High & low

Ecuador, in South America, is the only country in the **world** where the **temperature** reaches **zero** at **zero** degrees **latitude**. Although it sits right on the **equator**, you can see **icy glaciers** in its mountain peaks.

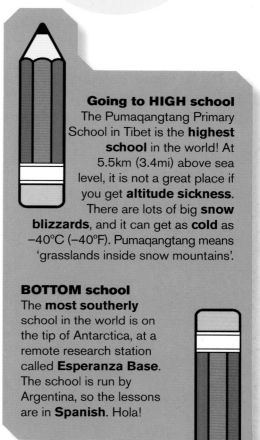

Going to HIGH school
The Pumaqangtang Primary School in Tibet is the **highest school** in the world! At 5.5km (3.4mi) above sea level, it is not a great place if you get **altitude sickness**. There are lots of big **snow blizzards**, and it can get as **cold** as −40°C (−40°F). Pumaqangtang means 'grasslands inside snow mountains'.

BOTTOM school
The **most southerly** school in the world is on the tip of Antarctica, at a remote research station called **Esperanza Base**. The school is run by Argentina, so the lessons are in **Spanish**. Hola!

POLES APART
As the crow flies, it's about **20,000km** (12,430mi) from the **North Pole** to **South Pole**.

Checking in
At **3962m** (13,000ft), the Everest View Hotel in Nepal is the **highest hotel** in the world.

High there

La Rinconada, Peru, is the world's **highest city**, **5098m** (16,728ft) above sea level. It's so high up that the tip of western Europe's highest mountain, **Mont Blanc**, would be 290m (950ft) **lower**.

KISS ME AND I'LL TURN INTO A PRINCE...

Volcano lizard

Pink land iguanas are **very rare**. They live only on the **Volcan Wolf volcano** in the **Galapagos Islands**.

Plump lump

The **Indian Purple Frog** was only discovered in **2003**. Scientists say it is a **living fossil**. It is also nicknamed the **pig-nose frog** or **doughnut frog**. Most of the time it **lives underground**.

Bloom bloom bloom

Every year, people in **Japan** eagerly await **cherry blossom season**. They love to **picnic under the trees**, in centuries-old **flower-viewing** ('hanami') **festivals**. From **March** to **May**, the flower blooms **sweep across** different parts of Japan. **TV news reports** even track the **cherry blossom front** ('sakura zensen'), as it **moves across** the country.

Furry scaly fairy story

The rare **pichiciego** from **Argentina** is one of the **most peculiar creatures ever**. It looks like a **furry hamster**, but it has a shell of **pink bony scales** along its back, and **pink scaly feet** with the **hugest claws**. Also called a **pink fairy armadillo**, it is the **smallest member** of the armadillo family, and will **fit in your hand**. When it is scared, it can **burrow into sand in seconds**, thanks to its massive claws.

Berry crazy

The **biggest purple berry** is actually eaten **all around the world** as a **vegetable**. The **eggplant**, or **aubergine**, is native to **India**, where it is known as **brinjal**. Back in the old days, people thought **eating it** made you **insane**.

Spikiest mouthful ever

Purple sea urchins are some of the **prickliest creatures** in the sea. They can **live** for up to **30 years**. **Otters** love to **dine** on them. **So do** people in **Japan** and **Sicily!**

Rosiest waters

The **world's pinkest lake** is **Lac Rose (Rose Lake)**, also called **Lake Retba**, in the African nation of **Senegal**. Its unusual pinkness is caused by **bacteria** that thrive in its **highly salty** waters. People **harvest salt** from the lake.

PINKEST & PURPLEST

BACK OFF OR I'LL BURP FROM MY OTHER END!

Pretty astonishing things come in shades of pink and purple

Happy snappy poo

Huge, heavy, pinky-purply hippos love **wallowing** in African waterholes to **stay cool**. Here's another cool thing about them: **hippo sweat is pink!** Hippos might look **cute and cuddly**, but these **hefty vegetarians kill more people** in Africa than any other large animal. If a hippo **yawns** and shows you its **huge pink throat** and **long sharp teeth, run for your life** – it is telling you it is **super cranky!** Those strong jaws can **bite a crocodile in half**. And if that doesn't **scare you off**, a hippo might pull a really **dirty trick** by **spraying poo all over you**.

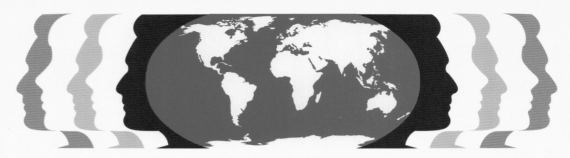

7 billion

That's how many people live on Planet Earth.

214,000

How much the Earth's human population is increasing every day.

PEOPLE POWER

Surprising statistics about us humans

Hey there pretty boys

The **Wodaabé people** in **Niger, Africa**, do things a little differently. **Instead of young ladies** going in **beauty contests,** it's the **young men** who **put on make-up** and their **finest threads**, during the **Cure Salée (Salt Cure) festival**, to try to find a **nice wife.**

LET'S FACE IT – IT'S TIME TO KISS AND MAKE UP!

5 most populated countries
1 China 1,347,350,000
2 India 1,210,193,422
3 United States 313,430,000
4 Indonesia 237,641,326
5 Brazil 192,376,496

5 least populated countries
1 Vatican City 800
2 Nauru 10,000
3 Tuvalu 10,000
4 Palau 21,000
5 San Marino 32,300

Long live the people
If you are born in the small European country of **Andorra**, you can expect to live for **82.4 years – longer than anywhere else** on Earth. The **next longest-living people** are the **Japanese,** who live on average for **82.2 years.**

We're all Rip Van Winkle
On average, **if you live to the age of 60**, you will have spent **more than 20 years asleep!**

Reach for the sky
The **Dutch** are the **world's tallest people.** Dutch men on average are **185cm (6ft 1in)**, while **Dutch women are 170cm (5ft 7in).**

World's shortest people
The **Mbuti**, from **Congo**, are **the shortest group of people** on Earth. Their average height is **137cm (4ft 6in).**

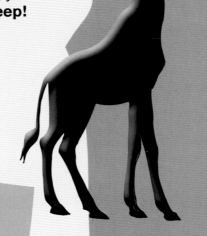

5–6m
(16–20ft)
Giraffe
Average height

185cm
(6ft 1in)
Dutch people
Average male height

137cm
(4ft 6in)
Mbuti people
Average male height

Go batty

Every evening in **summer**, more than **20 million bats** zoom out of **Bracken Cave in Texas** to feed. It takes **three hours** for all the tiny critters in the **world's largest bat colony** to get out of the cave. The **swarm** even shows up on the **radar** of the **local airport**. The hungry little Mexican free-tailed bats gobble down **250 tonnes (276 tons) of insects a night**.

Pirate treasure

Back in the **1600s**, **pirates** in the **Bahamas** really did hide treasures they stole from passing ships. Where? In **caves**, of course, in the thousands of islands that make up the Bahamas. **Who knows, some of it could still be hidden away!**

EMPIRE STATE BUILDING

COMING, READY OR NOT!

Do drop in

The **Vrtoglavica Cave** in **Slovenia** has the **world's deepest single vertical drop: 603m (1978ft)**. The **Empire State Building** in New York or the **Petronas Towers** in Malaysia would easily fit in it. However, the **Cave of Swallows** in **Mexico** is the **world's largest cave shaft**, because it is very wide, as well as **333m (1094ft) deep** – deep enough to swallow New York's **319m (1047ft) Chrysler Building**. People **BASE jump** into it.

CHRYSLER BUILDING

Crystal playgrounds

Climbing up and **down** and **around** the truly **giant** white crystals in **Mexico's Cave of Crystals** makes you feel really **tiny**. Some crystals are up to **11m (36ft) long** – six times longer than a tall man.

Black & smelly

A cave in **Romania**, discovered in 1986, is crawling with **blind spiders**, **scorpions**, **leeches** and **millipedes**, all sealed off and living in **complete darkness**. It's the only known **ecosystem** on land that **doesn't need sunlight**. The animals live on bacteria that get their energy from **rotten egg gas!**

INCREDIBLE CAVES

So much more than just a big hole in the ground ... some people even dive into them!

Ancient art

Chauvet Cave in **France** has the **oldest cave art in the world**. Some of the paintings on the walls are **32,000 years** old. It even has paintings of species that are **now extinct**, such as a **megaceros** (a huge elk) and **mammoths**.

MAKING A SPLASH!

A whole world of watery adventures

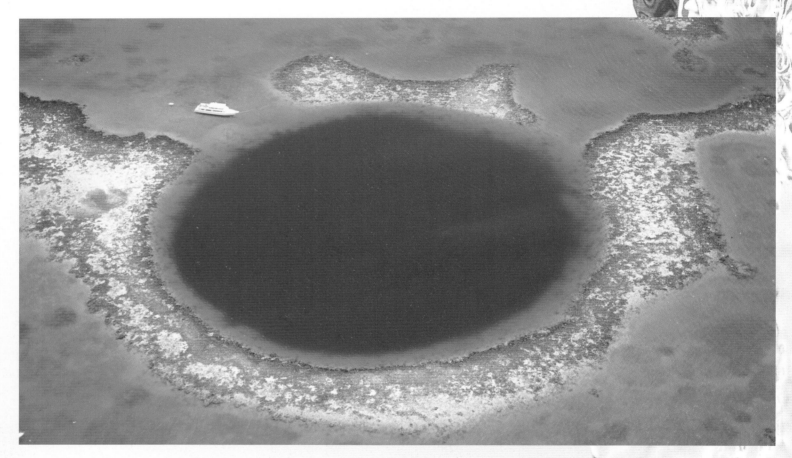

Blue holes all around

People love exploring the famous **'blue holes'** in our seas and oceans. These **deep round holes**, where the **ocean floor suddenly drops away**, are called **'sinkholes'**.

At the bottom of the beautiful **125m (410ft) Great Blue Hole** off **Belize** (pictured) are **natural underwater passageways**, where you can see **stalactites** and even **old fossils** – but to get there you **have to swim** through a **layer of poisonous gas.**

The **130m (426ft)** deep **Red Sea Blue Hole**, off the coast of **Egypt**, is famous for its **beautiful fish and coral**. It is also nicknamed the **'world's deadliest dive'** and **'diver's cemetery'**. At least **40 divers have died here**.

The **deepest seawater sinkhole** is the **202m (663ft) Dean's Blue Hole**, in the **Bahamas**, where people often **try to break** the **world free-diving record – 101m (331ft)** on a **single breath of air.**

Sharkiest dive

South Africa's Shark Alley is nicknamed the '**great white shark capital of the world'.** Here, **thrill-seekers** jump into **steel cages** off the side of boats to **go swimming** with **lots** of **awesomely big great white sharks.**

Swimming with crocs

Lake Argyle is **Australia's largest human-made lake**. And it's **full of crocodiles:** about **25,000 of them!** The crocs **don't usually eat people**, but they can give you a **nasty nip**. So when you are competing in the **world's biggest freshwater swimming marathon** – the **20km (12½mi) Lake Argyle Classic** – you might like to swim just that **little bit faster!**

Diving the icy rift

You'll need to put on a **very warm 'drysuit'** to go diving in **Iceland's famous Silfra Rift**. The **Silfra fissure** in Iceland's **Thingvellir National Park** is a great crack between the **two big tectonic plates** that sit underneath **Europe and North America**, like **giant 'bones'** in the **Earth**. You can actually dive in this deep crack, as parts of it are **full of water** that is **extremely pure and clear** – and only **just above freezing**. This crack is getting wider, as these **two tectonic plates** are **drifting** about **2cm (¾in)** further apart **every year**.

FAST FOOD HOME DELIVERY PLEASE!

Smelly bellies

North American **skunks** are famous for their **repulsive pong**. Whenever they feel threatened, they **aim their bottom** at the nearest offender, **raise their tail** and **squirt** a **diabolically stinky oily spray** at them, from up to **3m** (10ft) away. The **smell** can **linger** for **days**.

STAY AWAY OR I'LL SPRAY!

Bamboozle snoozer

China's shy and hugely cute **giant pandas** are one of the **world's rarest mammals**. They **love** to **eat**. They spend about **16 hours** a day **chowing down** on bamboo and, er, **more bamboo**. And when they are not eating, they are **usually asleep**.

I LOOK LIKE I'VE JUST SEEN A GHOST!

Tiger, tiger, burning white

White tigers are **rarely seen** in the **wild**. Usually they are seen only in zoos. Their very **unusual colouring** comes from a **genetic defect** from inbreeding.

Think of how white milk is, or a sheet of paper. That's nothing compared to the **ghost beetle**. This little bug from Southeast Asia is the **whitest natural object on Earth**. Scientists are studying it to learn how to make other things whiter and brighter.

The **blackest thing in the world** is a sheet of tiny carbon tubes, made in a US laboratory, that absorbs almost all light. It is **30 times blacker** than what scientists call 'black'.

Stop press!

What's **black** and **white** and **read all over**? A **newspaper**, of course. The **biggest-selling** newspaper in the world is *Yomiuri Shimbun*, from **Japan**, which sells more than **14 million copies** every day. About **520 million newspapers** are sold around the world every day. It takes **75,000 trees** to print one Sunday edition of *The New York Times*.

BLACK & WHITE

Sometimes the world really is black and white

Stripe me lucky

The **striped patterns** on zebras are **unique** to each zebra – just like **fingerprints**. These **wild African horses** have never really been tamed. They **sleep** standing up!

160 million years ago
That's sick!

Scientists in England discovered **vomit** from an **ichthyosaur** in Peterborough. **Ichthyosaurs** were **marine reptiles** that lived at the same time as dinosaurs, about **160 million years ago**. The dino **spew** was made up of the **remains of shellfish**.

Fowl tasting

If you want to find out what that terrifying dinosaur, **Tyrannosaurus rex**, would taste like, **eat a chicken**. That's because chickens are modern-day descendants of the T. rex!

MMM. DEAD TASTY!

TRAPPED IN TIME

Reminders of days long, long ago

We are all time travellers

Looking up at the sky at night is like looking into a **time machine**. The light we can see from **billions of stars** has often been travelling for **millions of years before it reaches Earth**. Perhaps some of the stars do not even exist anymore.

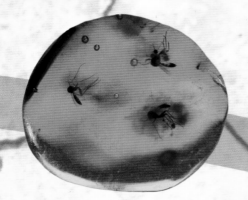

80 million years ago
Feathered find

A **thin strand of 'hair'** trapped in an **80-million-year-old** piece of **amber** found near **Alberta, Canada**, turned out to be the **world's first feather** from an **ancient bird**. You might also find **insects** trapped in amber, as well as **flowers** and **leaves**.

10,000 years ago
Mammoth task

The bodies of **woolly mammoths** that lived more than **10,000 years ago** have been found preserved in the **frozen soil** of **Siberia**. Scientists hope that one day they can **extract DNA** from the creatures and bring them back to life, in a real-life **Jurassic Park**.

4500 years ago
All wrapped up

Rich and **powerful people** in **Ancient Egypt** were **mummified** after they died, so they could travel to the afterlife. Their **organs were removed** through a **slit in the side of their body**, and their **brains were dragged out through** their **nose, using a long hook**. Then their bodies were **dried out** and wrapped in special sheets. Really important people such as **pharaohs** and **queens** were buried in **pyramids**, such as the **Great Pyramid of Giza**, in **Egypt**.

2500 years ago
Looking good for their age

The **bodies** of people found in **bogs** of northern Europe can be up to **2500 years old**, and often **perfectly preserved**. It appears that many of them were **murdered** before their bodies were thrown into the **swamps**.

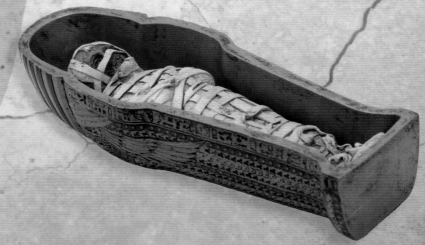

Dig for a swim

Hot Water Beach, on New Zealand's **Coromandel Peninsula**, is a great place for a dip **in the middle of winter**. Rather than swimming in the sea, beachgoers **dig holes in the sand**, which fill with **warm mineral waters**. They can then have a **nice warm soak**, no matter how cold the air temperature is.

Long drive, longer walk

It would take you **about a week** to **walk along the world's longest beach**. The beach, near **Cox's Bazaar**, in **Bangladesh**, is a **120km (75mi) strip of sand**. It is popular with locals, who crowd onto its golden sands throughout the year.

Rainbow beaches

The beaches of Harbour Island in the **Bahamas** have beautiful **pink sand,** thanks to the coral mixed through it. Vik Beach in **Iceland** is covered in volcanic **black sand** and **flat black stones** and **pebbles**; there are also eerie dark rocky outcrops sticking out of the water, like wicked witches' hats. Olivine crystals from a volcanic explosion are responsible for the **green sand** on **Hawaii's** Papakolea Beach. Then there's **Red Beach** on the Greek island of **Santorini**, which – you guessed it – has **red sand**. Minerals leaching onto Pfeiffer Beach in **California** have turned some of its **sand bright purple**.

That's plane crazy

You'd better be careful where you lie down if you go sunbathing at **Maho Beach**, on the island of **St Maarten** in the **Caribbean**. The island's **airport** is **right next to the beach** – and **huge planes** skim **just a few metres above the sand** while landing … often **blowing beachgoers** right **off their feet!**

LIFE'S A BEACH!

Relax and have a splash ...

Ocean under cover

If you are worried about sunburn, try having a swim at the world's **largest indoor beach**. Ocean Dome, in Miyazaki, southern Japan, is 300m (984ft) long and 100m (328ft) wide. Its roof has a beautiful **blue sky** painted on it, there's a **flame-spitting volcano** next to it, and the most perfect blue water laps onto **fake sand** that doesn't stick to you like the real stuff does.

Dinosaurs in the cliffs

Take a walk along the **Jurassic Coast**, in south-west **England**, and you are sure to come face to face with a **dinosaur**. The sea has washed away the land, leaving layer after layer of ancient fossils exposed. **The first pterodactyl** – a giant flying reptile – was found here.

Lots of pop

The **world's bubbliest beach** could very well be **Champagne Beach** in **Dominica**. Tiny bubbles rise constantly from the **volcanic sea floor**, creating an effect **like a glass of fizzy pop**. It's a great place to go **snorkelling**.

700,500,000,000,000,000,000

That's how many **grains of sand** there are on the **world's beaches**, according to **mathematicians** at the **University of Hawaii**. And that doesn't include the sand in any deserts!

175,000,000 litres
(46,000,000 gallons)

Every second of every day, this amount of water pours into the Atlantic Ocean from the Amazon. That's enough water to fill **70 Olympic swimming pools** (or **1.1 million bathtubs**) every second!

Extreme reversal

Once upon a time, the Amazon River **flowed in the opposite direction**, and emptied into the **Pacific Ocean**. But then, only about **65 million years ago**, the **Andes Mountains** started to grow, forcing the river to run the other way.

Scariest little fish

Piranhas are **ferocious fish** that live in the Amazon River. They are not very big, but they have **razor-sharp teeth** and like **eating meat**. When an **animal falls** into the river, **hundreds** of piranhas snap into a **feeding frenzy**, stripping the **flesh** off its bones in minutes.

MIGHTY AMAZON

One-fifth of all the fresh water entering **the world's oceans** comes from the Amazon.

The Amazon River in South America is the HUGEST river in the world!

Shock discovery

The **world's most shocking animal**, the **electric eel**, is not really an eel, but a knifefish. It can give you an electric shock of **500 volts**, which is **enough to kill you**. It uses its startling power to stun prey.

Ahoy there!

The floating village of **Belén** in **Peru** is nicknamed **'the Venice of the Amazon'**. Why? Because it floats! Why? Because the **Amazon River floods every year**. Many wooden homes are strapped to big poles so they don't float away. **Kids here paddle** to their **floating school**. The village even has a **floating disco**, **petrol station** and **shop**!

Do fly or sail in

Nearly 400,000 people live in the **rainforest city** of Iquitos, on the Amazon River in Peru. But you can't drive there. It is the **most populous city** in the world that you **cannot reach by road**. You can only arrive by boat or plane.

Pinkest thinkiest

Amazon River dolphins are **pretty pink** and **very smart**. Their brains are **40% larger than ours**. Their **long skinny beaks** let them hunt for **fish** among the **roots of trees** on the **edge of the river**. They turn brighter pink when they are surprised – a bit like when you blush!

6566 kilometres
(4080 miles)

The Amazon starts as a **tiny stream** high in the **Andes Mountains** in **Peru**, then flows through **Brazil's Amazon rainforest**, with **thousands of other rivers flowing into it**, until it reaches **the ocean**.

Really swell!

In February and March, during the **full Moon**, pororoca tidal waves surge up the Amazon River from the **Atlantic Ocean**, creating a **4m (13ft)** wall of water. **Crazy surfers** ignore the **snakes, piranhas and crocodiles** to ride these **huge brown** waves.

NEXT STOP, EUROPE!

Sun-bathing blob

The **mola mola** is the **heaviest** of all **bony fish**, and the **biggest blob afloat!** Big ones can be over **4m (14ft) long** and weigh up to **2235kg (4900lb)** – nearly as much as a **small truck**. They like to float around on top of the ocean, like they are sun-bathing, which is why they are **nicknamed 'sunfish'**. They love **eating jellyfish**, and females can carry **300 million eggs**. They don't mind hanging round the one area, although one mola mola cruised from the US **New England coastline** down to the **Caribbean** and **Gulf of Mexico**.

Taxi!

The **Gulf Stream** is a very **quick**, very **strong** current that runs through the **Atlantic Ocean** like a **70km (45mi) wide river**. It is one reason why it has always been **quicker to sail from America to Europe**, rather than the other way round. Lots of sea creatures, such as **turtles**, use it like a super-speedy **'taxi service'** to travel across the oceans. **Wheee!**

OCEAN WANDERERS

The most amazing creatures cruise our oceans

No fluke!

Whales are great **ocean cruisers**.

Every year, **grey whales** glide up and down the US west coast for more than **8000km (5000mi)** each way between **cold feeding waters** and **warm breeding waters**.

Great white torpedoes

Look out for the **biggest predatory fish in the ocean**: yes, it's the **great white shark!** They can grow **6m (20ft) long**, and weigh up to **2250kg (5000lb). Despite their size**, they can **zoom through the water** at up to **24km/h (15mph)**, thanks to their **powerful tails**. Some of them make **mighty solo journeys** across the oceans. One tagged shark swam from the bottom of **South Africa** to the coast of **Western Australia**: about **11,000km (6835mi)** in **99** days. They get blamed for lots of shark attacks – but **humans are really not their favourite snack**.

WHO NEEDS THE DENTIST?

Gentlest of giants

The majestic **whale shark** is the **most humungous non-bony fish** in the **world!** Looking more like a **whale** than a **shark**, it can grow **as long as a bus**. The **largest one** ever seen stretched over **12m (41ft)** and weighed over **21.5 tonnes (47,000lb)**. They slowly cruise around warm oceans – one clocked up a **13,000km (8078mi)** journey **over three years**. Whale sharks have **thousands of teeth** – but these are **so tiny** (only 3mm/0.1in wide) that they can only eat **little shrimp** and **plankton**. They can live up to **100 years**.

12 metres

NOW FOR MY NEXT MAGNIFICENT OCEAN ADVENTURE!

The **record** goes to a **humpback whale** that cruised more than **9800km (6000mi)**.

Brazil

Madagascar

(9800km)

It travelled from **Brazil** to **Madagascar** – the **longest mammal migration** ever recorded.

What colossal giants!

There are many **old tales** about **giant octopuses attacking ships**, including ancient **Norse legends** about the **kraken**, a **huge sea monster** that **pulled ships under water**. In real life, **two enormous tentacular** relatives really do dwell in the depths: **the giant squid** and **colossal squid**. Each can grow **as long as a school bus**. **One colossal squid** weighed a whopping **495kg (1091lb)!** Colossal squid have **the world's biggest eyeballs** – each one is **bigger than a dinner plate**. Their **strong**, **beak-like mouth** can cut through **steel cable**. Both squids dive as deep as **2000m (6500ft)**, looking for something to grab with their **eight arms** and **two incredibly long tentacles**. **Colossal squid** even grapple with **sperm whales!**

Gulp!

More **mouth** than body, the **gulper eel** can **swallow** an animal **much bigger than itself** because of its **immense, gaping hungry jaws** and **ultra-stretchy skinny belly**. It is usually black or green, and its **long skinny tail** lures in prey by **flashing pink** or **red**.

Other bizarre deep sea creatures

Hagfish, snot fish, **viper fish,** goblin shark, **sea pig,** rat-tail, **spook fish,** blob fish, **coffin fish,** angler fish, **hatchet fish,** dumbo octopus, **yeti crab,** giant isopod, **giant sea spider** ...

Dracula's cousin

Here's a **velvety black, blue-blooded blob** with a fearsome Latin name: **Vampyroteuthis infernalis** – the **'vampire squid from hell'**. It slowly **'flies'** through the water with its mysterious **'cape'**, looking around with **huge glowing red** or **blue eyes**. Lucky it is only **as long as a ruler!** Its **eight arms** are like a **cloak**, connected by a **web of skin**, lined with **rows of tooth-like spines**. When scared, it **draws its arms over its head** and completely **covers itself with its spiny cloak**. Compared to the **size of its head**, it has the **biggest eyes in the animal kingdom**. If we had eyes their size, they would **be as big as beach balls!**

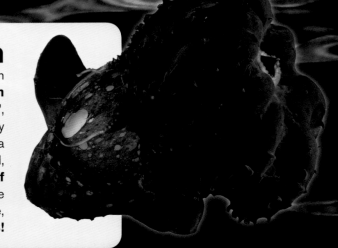

> MUM ALWAYS TELLS ME TO EAT WITH MY MOUTH OPEN!

Fang you very much

For its size, the **scary little fangtooth** has the **largest teeth in the ocean**. It can't even close its mouth, its **teeth are so big!** It is covered in **small prickly scales** and **knobby bits**.

MONSTERS OF THE DEEP

In our deepest oceans dwell the weirdest creatures ever

Why are lots of deep sea animals red?

In low light, red looks black, so being red makes them 'invisible'.

Number of people who have walked on the Moon

Number who have been to the deepest part of the ocean

Welcome to planet water

About **70% of planet Earth** is actually **under the ocean!** Nearly **half of the ocean** is over **3km (9800ft) deep**. And some bits are **over three times as deep again**. Our **deepest oceans** are still **largely unexplored. More people have travelled into space** than to the **bottom** of the **deepest ocean**. We know more about the **Moon** than our **deep blue seas**. But we do know it's a **whole new world down there**. It's **pitch black, dreadfully cold**, and the **extreme pressure** of all that water sitting on top is **lung-crushing** and **suffocating**. The **deep abyss** is the **world's largest habitat**, full of the **strangest sea creatures** that **look like aliens** from **outer space**. Some of them are **see-through**, and many of them have **huge bulging eyes, big razor-sharp teeth** and **flashing lights** to lure you in!

On a web and a prayer

Spiders not only **spin webs** to **catch flies** – they also use them **to go flying!** These **adventurous arachnids spin little parachutes** which **ride on the wind**, carrying the spider with them. Some spiders have been caught in **ships' sails 1600km (1000mi)** from land. Others have been detected by **weather balloons 5000m** (16,000ft) in the air!

Big blow

The **highest wind speed** ever recorded was **408km/h** (253mph), on **10 April 1996**, during **tropical cyclone Olivia**. That's **faster than a bullet train** on **a long straight track**. It was at a weather station on **Barrow Island**, off the coast of Western Australia.

WIND POWER

The air we breathe can be furiously strong!

PARDON ME...

Forty million tonnes of Sahara Desert dust is **blown across the Atlantic Ocean** every year. Without it, the **Amazon rainforest** would be **much less fertile**.

Master blaster

Paul Oldfield, from **England,** might have the **best job in the world – people pay him to let rip**. He's better known as **Mr Methane,** and he says he's the world's only **professional farter (or 'flatulist')**. During his stage show he performs **classical** and **rock music** with **his bottom, blows out candles** and **inflates balloons**.

UP, UP AND AWAY!

Vicious cycle

A **tropical cyclone** forms when **warm air** from the **surface of the ocean** gets **sucked up** into **cooler air above**, kind of like up a chimney. **Surrounding air rushes in** to take its place; it also becomes **warm and moist,** and **rises too**. **Massive** amounts of energy are created. Scientists say **the amount of energy in a tropical cyclone** is equal to exploding a **10-megaton nuclear bomb every 20 minutes**, or **11,000 Hiroshima bombs**.

FRANCE

Alley catastrophe

A **huge stretch of land** between the **Rocky Mountains** and the **Appalachian Mountains** in the US is known as **Tornado Alley**. Here, **hundreds of tornadoes** – **wildly twisting funnels of wind** moving at up to **400km/h** (250mph), and **the world's most violent storms** – tear **paths of destruction** every year.

Restless seas

In the deserts of **north Africa**, the wind helps create endlessly shifting **seas of sand**, called **ergs,** full of **towering dunes**. The **world's largest** erg is the **Rub' al Khali**. Located in **Saudi Arabia, Yemen, Oman** and the **United Arab Emirates**, it covers an area **greater than France** – more than **600,000 sq km** (230,000 sq mi).

In a spin

Every year, in **December**, more than a **million people** go to the **whirling dervish festival** in Konya, **Turkey**, to watch devout dancers wearing **long white skirts** and a **flowerpot-style hat** **whirl** and **twirl** themselves, **faster** and **faster**, into a divine **trance**.

Dancing dragons, prancing lions

Chinese New Year is one of the **biggest, brightest** and **noisiest** celebrations around, and is held in Chinatowns **all over the world**. Everyone loves the colourful **street dances**, where **leaping lions** and **huge dragons** parade to **noisy drums, gongs** and **cymbals, scaring off evil spirits** and bringing **good luck**. In the **Dragon Dance**, a **team** of dancers holds up a **long dragon** – the **longer** the dragon, the **luckier**.

Hope that hanky is clean

What are those **silly grown-ups** doing, **dressed in white**, with **bells** around their **legs** and **flowers** on their **hats, leaping around** and **waving giant white hankies** or **sticks in the air?** Actually, they are doing a charming old **English folk dance**, the **Morris dance**!

HOPE THE WIND DOESN'T CHANGE DIRECTION!

Haka haka who?

The **Maori haka** is one of the **scariest** dances around! **New Zealand's All Blacks** rugby team do a haka before each game, **glaring, stomping, chanting** and **poking out** their **tongues** to turn their **opponents to jelly**. However, some haka dances are performed to **welcome** visitors, not **scare** them.

Big tribal showdown

Tribes in **Papua New Guinea** love to get together and compete in a big **'sing-sing'**. They **paint themselves up**, put on their **wildest outfits** and **sing and dance**. Two huge sing-sings bring in up to a **hundred tribes** from all over the country: the **Mt Hagen Show** in August, and the **Goroka Show** in September. The **tribal dances** are especially spectacular.

I'M OFF TO PAINT THE TOWN RED... AND YELLOW

MOVE IT!

Shake, wiggle, shimmy and stomp to all those crazy beats

FALLING DOESN'T WORRY ME, IT'S THE SUDDEN STOP AT THE END THAT HURTS!

This is crazy

The **fastest sport on Earth**, without using an engine, is **downhill speed skiing**. Brave (or crazy) skiers **tuck themselves up tight** and **race down steep snowy hills** at up to **251km/h (156mph)**. In 1997, American **Jeff Hamilton** fell off at **243km/h (151mph)**. Amazingly, he shattered only **three small bones** – but he did get terrible **'snow burn'**.

Lot of bull

The world's **'fastest festival'** could be **San Fermin**, held every July in **Pamplona, Spain**. It is certainly **one of the deadliest!** A whole lot of men, **dressed in white**, are chased through narrow streets by **mad bulls wearing clanking cowbells**. Since **1910**, at least **16 people** have been **killed** during **'the running of the bulls'**, and **200 badly injured**.

NEED FOR SPEED

Things that go really FAST!

THE LAST TIME I WENT THIS FAST, ALL MY BEAUTIFUL SPOTS BLEW OFF!

How fast is a cheetah?

Cheetah: 100m (109yd) in **6.13 seconds**

Athlete: 100m (109yd) in **9.6 seconds**

Cheetah: 0–100km/h (60mph) in **3 seconds**

Ferrari: 0–100km/h (60mph) in **3 seconds**

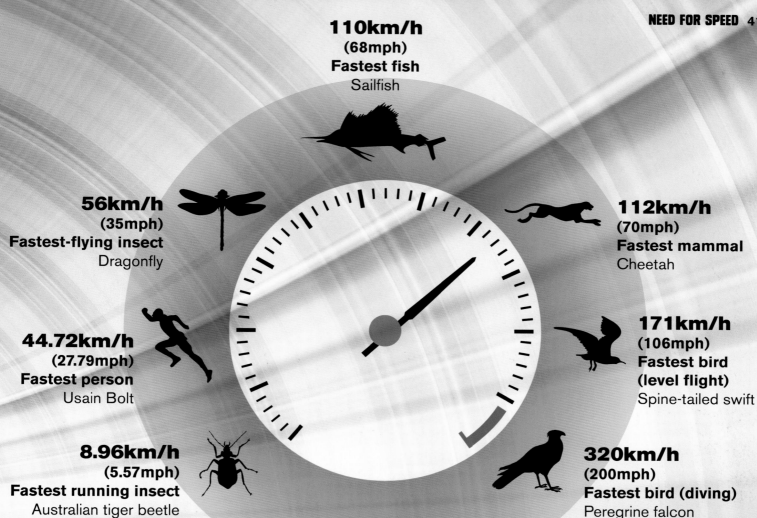

110km/h
(68mph)
Fastest fish
Sailfish

56km/h
(35mph)
Fastest-flying insect
Dragonfly

112km/h
(70mph)
Fastest mammal
Cheetah

44.72km/h
(27.79mph)
Fastest person
Usain Bolt

171km/h
(106mph)
Fastest bird
(level flight)
Spine-tailed swift

8.96km/h
(5.57mph)
Fastest running insect
Australian tiger beetle

320km/h
(200mph)
Fastest bird (diving)
Peregrine falcon

The fastest living things

SIX-LEGGED SPEEDSTER: The fastest-running insect is the **Australian tiger beetle**, which has been clocked travelling at **8.96km/h (5.57mph)**. That may not sound fast, but that's about **170 body lengths per second**. Or you running at **550km/h (340mph)**! **A BLUR OF FUR:** Imagine that you are the **fastest sprinter in the world**. If you were trying to **escape a cheetah** in the **Namibian** savannah and the nearest tree you could climb was **100m (328ft) away**, the cheetah would **beat you there**, even if it was **twice as far away** when you both started running. You'd have to be **driving a sports car** to come close to the **big cat's acceleration**. Fortunately, a cheetah is much more likely to run away from you! **FLEET FISH: Sailfish** are the **ocean kings and queens of speed**. These **3m (10ft)** fish can swim at **110km/h (68mph)**. They use the **huge sail** that runs along their back to make themselves look even bigger, **scaring little fish** together into larger herds to gobble up. Sailfish have another **nifty trick**: they can also **instantly change their colour** to confuse their prey. **FLASH CANNIBAL FALCON:** Lucky you are not a bird, or you might be in the penetrating sights of a **peregrine falcon**. These **speedy hunters** like to catch other birds while they're flying, swooping down on them at **320km/h (200mph)**. They are the **fastest birds** and the **fastest animals in the world**.

Fiery night show

Kilauea, in **Hawaii**, is the **world's most active volcano**, and when the sun goes down it is **Kilauea's turn to shine**. Rivers of **red lava glow brightly in the dark**, and sometimes the **red-hot lava spurts high into the air** from **steaming holes in the earth**. Some of the lava even **pours into the sea**. Other lava bits are slowly **swallowing roads and houses**.

Most dazzling brilliance

Physicists in Texas have created **the brightest light in the universe**. They used a **super-powerful laser** to make a **very brief pulse of light** with an intensity of **1 million billion watts** – more than the **output of all the world's power stations combined**. The laser is kept at the **University of Texas**. **Don't look down the pointy end when it's on**.

Lady luck loves lamps

Diwali is a huge **Hindu festival** celebrated throughout the world. It is known as the **Festival of Lights** because people **light small lamps** and **let off firecrackers** to celebrate the **triumph of good over evil**. In **India**, the **lighted lamps** help the **goddess of wealth**, **Lakshmi**, find her way into people's homes.

Who needs a torch?

Before there were **battery-powered torches**, some people used **glowing mushrooms** to find their way in the dark. No one is really sure why the **fungus glows bright neon green** in the dark, but scientists think it might be to **attract insects** that help the **fungi reproduce**. They grow in many places throughout the world, but are very abundant in **Japan** and **Brazil**. So next time you're walking through a forest at night, **turn off your torch** – you might spot an **eerie green glow** in the distance.

LET THERE BE LIGHT

Putting on a blazing good show …

That's a lot of candles

A **beam of light** shining out of the **Luxor Las Vegas Casino** is as bright as **42.3 billion candles**. The **light beam** is visible from **400km (250mi)** away, and can even be seen **from outer space**. A person floating **16km (10mi)** in the air above it could **easily read a book by the light**.

STOP! OR I'LL INK!

Escape artists

The **bright-red deep sea shrimp** has an extremely startling way of **escaping its enemies** – it **squirts out a glowing blue ooze** that **confuses its attacker**, giving it time to **sneak away to safety**. **Octopuses** pull off a similar trick when they **squirt black ink** into the faces of **unsuspecting** predators.

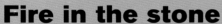

Fire in the stone

About **95% of the world's opals** come from the hot outback areas of **Australia**, such as **Lightning Ridge** and **Coober Pedy**. Opals are special for their **glowing colours**. The most valuable uncut opal is the **Olympic Australis Opal**, valued at around **AUD$2.5 million**. It weighs **3.45kg (7.5lb)**. The largest polished opal is the **Galaxy Opal**, which was found in **Brazil**. It was cut from a chunk of opal **the size of a grapefruit**.

Lights fantastic

The night sky near the **North** and **South poles** (pictured) often shimmers with curtains of **bright green**, **blue**, **purple** and **red lights**. These lights in the sky are called the **Northern and Southern lights**, or **auroras**, and they are two of **nature's most beautiful displays**. The sky lights up when the **Earth's atmosphere** interacts with **particles from the Sun**.

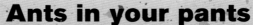

Ants in your pants

In the **five-day Entroido festival** in **Laza**, **Spain**, people put on **colourful costumes** and do **crazy things**. The **craziest thing** is that they collect **dirt filled with ants**, **sprinkle** the ants **with vinegar** to make them **really cranky**, then **fling the dirt and ants at people**, along with **muddy rags**, **ash**, **flour**, **water** … **Definitely don't try this at home**.

Singapore is probably **the world's cleanest city**. Anyone who gets caught **littering** or **spitting** or **selling chewing gum** has to **pay** a lot of **money**!

Spring rainbow

Hindu people in **India**, **Nepal**, **Pakistan** and **Bangladesh** celebrate **the start of spring** with the **Holi festival** – also known as the **'Festival of Colours'**. Kids especially have **great fun** throwing **brightly coloured powder** and **water** all over everyone, while yelling out **'Holi hai!'** Soon everybody ends up **rainbow coloured**.

MESSIEST

Don't look Mum, we're just having fun!

Biggest cold and flu fighters

More than **360 tonnes** (400 tons) **of oranges** are thrown in **February** during the **Battle of the Oranges**, in the Italian town of **Ivrea**. There's a **parade with horses and carriages** and townsfolk in **traditional outfits**, then **nine teams of people** hurl oranges at each other. If you wear a **red hat,** you're safe – but it also means **you can't throw an orange at anyone else**. Some streets get so full of **smashed, squishy, slippery oranges** that they have to bring **tractors** in to **clear some of the mess away**.

Splat!

The Spanish town of **Bunol** is famous for one **very big** and **very messy food fight**: the **La Tomatina festival**. Every year, in **August**, trucks carrying about **150,000 over-ripe tomatoes** turn up. **A shot rings out** and **it's on!** For **one crazy hour**, about **20,000 people** pelt each other with **sloppy tomatoes** and make the **biggest mess ever**. Finally **another shot is fired**, and then **fire trucks hose** the streets down … better take some **eye goggles!** If that's not **enough mess**, there's also a **tomato-flinging festival** in **Colombia**, called the **Tomatina Colombiana**, held in **June**, in the town of **Sutamarchan**.

FOR PEAT'S SAKE, WHAT WAS THAT? THIS IS THE FILTHIEST CONTEST EVER!

The mind boggles

Put on your **mask, snorkel and flippers**, hop in a **dark, smelly, muddy peat bog**, dog-paddle and kick **55m** (60yd) through **slimy weeds** and **leeches** – then turn around and do another lap, as quick as you can. That's what you have to do to win the **World Bog Snorkelling Championship**, at the Waen Rhydd peat bog in **Wales, UK**. The current **world record** is **84 seconds**. There's also the World **Mountain Bike Bog Snorkelling** Championships and the **Bog Snorkelling Triathlon** to try.

Flying feathers

Love a good pillow fight? Don't miss **International Pillow Fight Day**, which is held every year in **more than a hundred cities** around the **world**, every **March** or **April**. It can last a **few minutes** or a **few hours**, and starts when a siren or whistle blows.

Water, water everywhere

After all that **messing around**, you might need a **good wash** – and there's no better way than joining in **the world's biggest water fight**. To welcome in the **Thai New Year**, or **Songkran**, people all over **Thailand** wash away the old year by **splashing water over everyone using buckets, hoses, water guns** … and sometimes even **elephants!**

Art that grabs you

Is that a giant buried in the sand?
No, it's just a **giant's hand**. The **Mano de Desierto** (Hand of the Desert) is a big **sculpture** of **four fingers and a thumb** in Chile's **Atacama Desert**, made by **Chilean artist** Mario Irarrázabal. He also buried another hand in **Brava Beach, Uruguay**, which he called Monumento al Ahogado (**Monument to the Drowned**).

Massive mystery

About **1500 years ago**, people in **Peru** scraped **long trenches** in a **rocky desert** to create the mysterious **Nazca Lines**. The lines are dug in the shape of hundreds of **huge animals** and **plants**, such as **hummingbirds**, **monkeys**, **fish** and **lizards** – some more than **270m** (890ft) across. The **Nazca Lines** are the **world's largest geoglyphs**. Some people think they are **messages** to **aliens**, because you can **only see** the shapes **from the air**.

Having the biggest time

Australia is a **big country**, and its people have a **big** sense of **humour**, so they like to build lots of hugely silly **Big Things** … such as The Big **Banana**, The Big **Pineapple**, The Big **Golden Guitar**, The Big **Prawn**, The Big **Lobster**, The Big **Boxing Crocodile** and The Big **Merino** – a huge horned sheep made of concrete. Most have **some connection** to a **nearby town**. There are more than **150** Big Things across the country. Some have appeared on **stamps**, and many have starred in **movies** and **TV shows**.

> I REALLY SHOULD GET MY OWN DRIVER'S LICENCE!

All the emperor's men, and more

Unearthed in **1974**, China's **'terracotta army'** was one of the **biggest archaeological finds ever**. The **army** is actually a collection of **over 8000** clay **sculptures** that was **buried** with the **emperor Qin Shihuang** some **2200 years ago**. His **tomb** and **life-size soldiers** took **700,000 people** almost **40 years** to build. Each soldier has a **unique face**, just like in **real life**. There are also **130 chariots** and **670 horses**.

SUPER-SIZE

Extremely oversized attractions from around the world

Walking inside dinosaurs

The **world's largest dinosaurs** still stand in the deserts of **California**. The **Cabazon dinosaurs** are a pair of **concrete monsters** built in the **1960s** as a **tourist attraction**. One is a **Tyrannosaurus rex** and the other is a **larger-than-life Apatosaurus**. You can **climb into both of them** and **look out through their mouths**.

COME ON UP KIDS FOR A 'KILLER' VIEW ... JUST DON'T TICKLE MY THROAT OR I'LL SNEEZE!

Wheely high

The **Singapore Flyer** is a great way to get a **bird's-eye view** of that **exciting city**. The Flyer is the **world's tallest ferris wheel**. When you're at the **top of the wheel** you are a dizzying **165m (541ft) above the ground** – as high as a **50-storey building**.

High and dry
It's hard to believe that **this boat once hauled in fish** from the **Aral Sea**, which lies between **Kazakhstan** and **Uzbekistan**. But the **sea has been shrinking**, leaving boats such as this **marooned on dry land** – some more than **100km** (60mi) from **the water's edge**.

Hot to trot
The **world's toughest footrace** takes place every **July** in **Death Valley, California**. The **Badwater Ultramarathon** is a **217km (135mi)** race through **one of the hottest deserts in the world**, where temperatures often hit **50°C (122°F) in the shade**. About **80 people** take part each year, but about **one-third don't finish**. You **win a belt buckle** if you finish in **less than 48 hours**.

I REALLY WANT THAT BELT BUCKLE!

DESERTS
Our driest spots are dazzlingly different

WHERE IN BLAZES AM I?

An ice surprise
Although it's **freezing cold** and **permanently packed with ice**, **Antarctica** is also the **largest desert in the world**! The **Antarctic desert** covers an area of **13.8 million sq km** (5.3 million sq mi), which is much larger than **Europe, the US**, or **Australia**. It is called a desert because it receives **less than 250mm** (10in) of rain each year.

Got the chop
What are the chances? **The world's loneliest tree** was more than **400km (250mi)** from any other tree (that's about **a one-month walk**), but that didn't stop a **drunk driver** from **knocking it down with his truck** in 1973. A **steel monument** now stands in the **Sahara Desert** in **Niger** where the **Tree of Ténéré** once grew.

IT'S MY TURN TO BE ON LOOKOUT DUTY...

50°C
(122°F)
Sahara Desert (daytime)

40°C
(104°F)
Gobi Desert (summer)

−40°C
(−40°F)
Gobi Desert (winter)

Dangerous drink
Thousands of **thirsty camels** risk a **horrible death** when they take a drink at **Guelta d'Archei** in **Chad**. Lurking in its **life-giving waters** are lots of **hungry crocodiles**! A **guelta** is a **waterhole** that forms in the **desert** from underground springs.

Not all deserts are barren. The **Sonoran Desert** in **North America** has more than **2000 plant species**, and over **550 different species of mammals, birds, amphibians, reptiles, fish** and **insects.**

324m (1063ft)
Eiffel Tower

93m (305ft)
Statue of Liberty

465m (1526ft)
Isaouane-n-Tifernine

Grand sands
When the **wind blows** across the **vast sandy deserts of north Africa**, it creates huge seas of sand that look like a **giant golden ocean**. These big **'waves'** of sand are called **dunes**. Some of **the world's tallest sand dunes** are in a part of the **Sahara Desert** called **Isaouane-n-Tifernine** in **Algeria**, and are up to **465m (1526ft) tall**. Imagine trying to climb them!

Many animals in one

The **mimic octopus**, which lives in the sea off the **Indonesian coast**, is one of **the world's greatest tricksters**. The octopus **can change its shape, colour** and **movements to copy** more than **15 different dangerous marine animals.** It can make itself look like **a giant crab**, **a lionfish**, **a stingray** and even **a banded sea snake!** It changes its look to try to **scare off predators**.

Split personality

During **mating season**, **cuttlefish** develop **a split personality**. During the day, **the skins** of **male cuttlefish flash** in **bright contrasting patterns** and **colours** to **impress the ladies** and **warn off rivals**. But at night they use **their colourful skin skills** to **hide from predators**, by mimicking the colour, shape and texture of their surroundings. So if they hide **near a rock at night**, they will be the same **colour and texture** as rock. Or they'll look just like **sand** if they are **resting on the ocean floor**.

Sole survivor

Flat fish, such as **sole**, grow **both eyes** on **one side of their body!** They sit on the **bottom of the sea** and **keep a lookout** with both eyes for things that might **gobble them up**. It looks like they are lying **on their belly**, but they are really lying **on one side**.

NOTHING TO SEE HERE, HONEST

See-through skin

A chameleon's skin is see-through. It is the **cells underneath** its skin that let a chameleon **change its colour**. While chameleons sometimes change their colour **to blend in** with their **surroundings**, the colour changes are used mainly for **communication**. A calm chameleon might be **green**, while an angry chameleon might be **yellow** or **orange**. They can also do **weird things with their eyes**. Each one can **move by itself**, so chameleons can look in a few directions at once. **They really do have eyes in the back of their head!**

Stick with it

Stick insects are brilliant at **melting into their surroundings**. Their **bodies** and **legs** look just like **sticks** and **twigs**. Because the insects look like plants, **predators just ignore them**.

HEY, WHERE DID EVERYONE GO?

That's all white

Polar bears can't change their colour – but that doesn't matter, because **they live in places that are usually always snow white**! Being white makes it easy for polar bears to **sneak up on prey**. They also have an **amazingly sharp sense of smell** – they can even **sniff out animals** hiding **below the ice**.

NOT WHAT IT SEEMS

Extremely canny survival tactics

Razzle dazzle

Some animals use **a type of camouflage** called **dazzle**. **Zebras' stripes** are an example of this. When **zebras in herds run from a predator**, their stripes make it hard for the predator **to judge the zebras' speed** and **direction**, making it more likely they can escape. However, this type of camouflage makes them **easier to spot when standing still**.

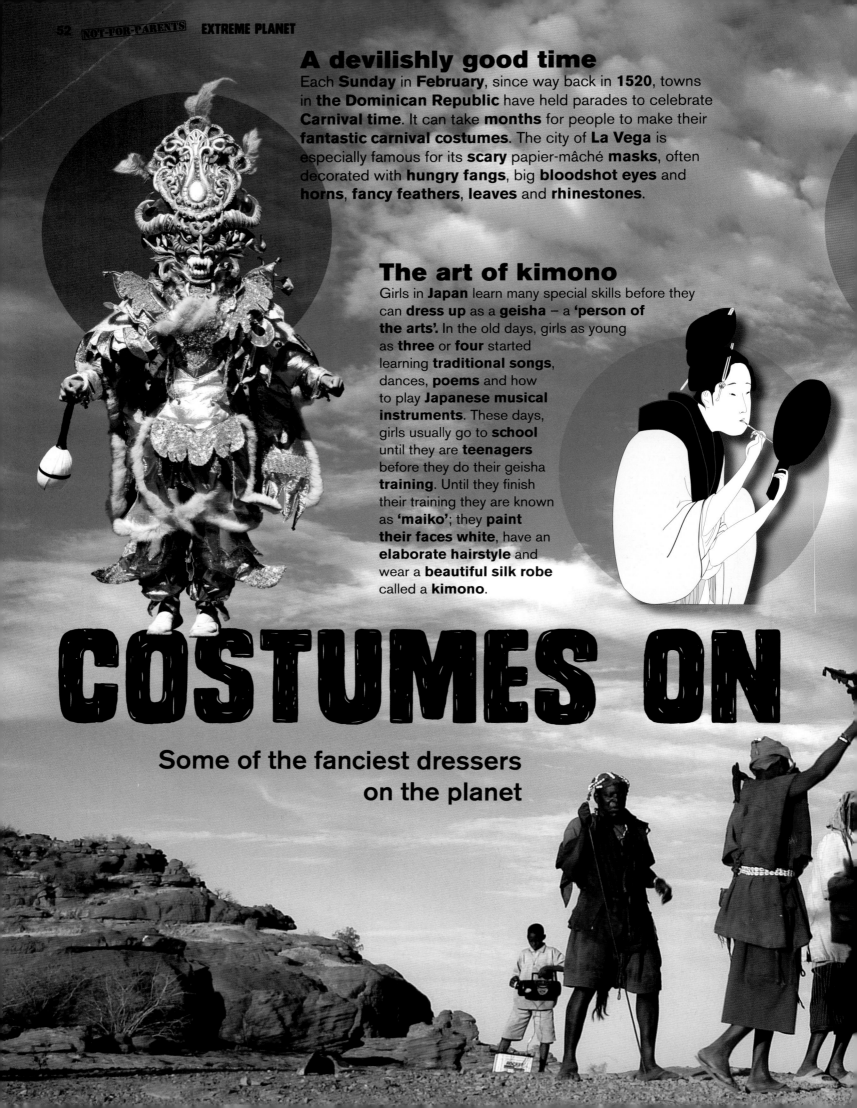

A devilishly good time

Each **Sunday** in **February**, since way back in **1520**, towns in **the Dominican Republic** have held parades to celebrate **Carnival time**. It can take **months** for people to make their **fantastic carnival costumes**. The city of **La Vega** is especially famous for its **scary** papier-mâché **masks**, often decorated with **hungry fangs**, big **bloodshot eyes** and **horns**, **fancy feathers**, **leaves** and **rhinestones**.

The art of kimono

Girls in **Japan** learn many special skills before they can **dress up** as a **geisha** – a **'person of the arts'**. In the old days, girls as young as **three** or **four** started learning **traditional songs**, dances, **poems** and how to play **Japanese musical instruments**. These days, girls usually go to **school** until they are **teenagers** before they do their geisha **training**. Until they finish their training they are known as **'maiko'**; they **paint their faces white**, have an **elaborate hairstyle** and wear a **beautiful silk robe** called a **kimono**.

COSTUMES ON

Some of the fanciest dressers on the planet

Lucky gilles

Boys in the Belgian town of **Binche** grow up hoping to be a **gille**. A gille is a **clown-like performer** who wears a **fancy costume** around **Easter** – a **wax mask**, a **colourful outfit** with **lacy white frills** around the **neck**, **wrists** and **ankles**, **wooden shoes** and **bells on their belt**. On the **final day** of the **Carnival of Binche**, they dance to **drums at dawn** and **wave bunches of sticks** to keep away **evil spirits**. Later they put on huge white **ostrich-feather hats** and up to **1000 gilles parade through the streets**, each one carrying **a basket of oranges**. They throw the oranges to people for **good luck.** Not everyone can be a gille, as the **outfits** are very **expensive**.

LOOK OUT EVIL SPIRITS, THIS IS A STICK-UP!

Having a ball

For **10 days each year**, usually in **February**, the Italian city of **Venice** has a **huge dress-up party** called the **Carnival of Venice**. People put on **amazing masks and costumes** and go **dancing at masked balls**, and the streets are full of **acrobats**, **musicians**, **magicians**, **clowns** and **puppeteers**. The carnival has been going **at least 800 years**.

Head for the sky

Imagine balancing a 6m (20ft) long **wooden mask on your teeth!** You have to be a **very strong** man from the **Dogon** tribe in **Mali**, **Africa**, to put on one of these long, thin **spirit masks**. These **masks** are **only worn** during special **funerals**. They are meant to connect **the heavens** with **the Earth**.

NOW, WHERE DID I LEAVE MY HAT?

Weird and wonderful

The **giraffe weevil** is not only a **weird-looking thing**, it also probably has **the longest head of any insect**. This strange insect is from the island of **Madagascar**. The **male weevil nods his big head around** to try to interest a mate, while the **ladies roll a leaf around their head** before **laying eggs in the leaf**.

Male fairyfly magnified 100 times

Can't see me, can't see you

The **smallest insects** are **male fairyflies**. These tiny wasps from **Costa Rica** grow to only **0.14mm (1/200in)** – **much smaller than a grain of salt**. They have **no wings, can't see**, and **they live on the eggs** of other insects. **Lady** wasps are **twice** as big as **males**.

BUG'S LIFE

Strangest facts about these most curious critters

Taken for a ride

Before a **jewel wasp** lays its eggs, it has to take **a cockroach for a ride!** This **colourful insect stings a cockroach** to make it sleepy, **bites off half its antennae**, then **rides the cockroach into the cockroach's burrow**, steering it in **with its long antennae**, sort of like **riding a horse**. The wasp then **lays its eggs in the cockroach's stomach** and **shuts it in the burrow with rocks** until the eggs hatch.

HERE, LET ME TAKE THAT FOR YOU …

Feats of strength

The **hercules beetle** is **so strong** it can lift **850 times its own body weight**. That would be like **us lifting an army tank** or **a giant dinosaur**.

Too many to count

It seems impossible, but scientists reckon that **most of the insect species** on the planet **still haven't been discovered!** They believe there are more than **9 million** different types of insects – that's **75% of all animal species**. People are **discovering a new type of insect,** on average, **every hour!**

WHAT'S UP DOC?

Weta whopper!

The largest insect in the world is so big it eats carrots! But it is also **very rare**. The **weta** is found only on **Little Barrier Island** in **New Zealand**. It looks a little bit like a **huge grasshopper**. It can weigh up to **70g (2.5oz)**, about the same as **three mice!** Its body can be **100mm (4in) long**.

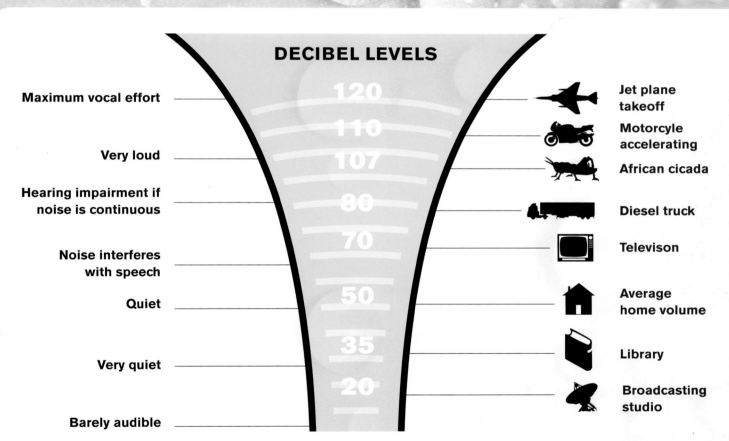

DECIBEL LEVELS

Maximum vocal effort — 120 — Jet plane takeoff

110 — Motorcyle accelerating

Very loud — 107 — African cicada

Hearing impairment if noise is continuous — 80 — Diesel truck

70 — Televison

Noise interferes with speech —

Quiet — 50 — Average home volume

35 — Library

Very quiet —

20 — Broadcasting studio

Barely audible —

NATURE'S CONCERT

Insects usually make sounds by **rubbing bits of themselves together**. And these sounds can often be **quite loud**. Think of when **thousands of cicadas** or **crickets** decide to make a racket **all at once** – the sound is **almost deafening! Cicadas are the loudest of all insects**, and the loudest cicada is the **African cicada**. It can blast out a tune at **107 decibels** – **that's as loud as a motorbike or a rock concert!**

Hotter than the Sun

The highest temperature ever recorded on Earth was produced in **Sandia National Laboratories** in California. The temperature of **2 billion °C (3.6 billion °F)** was created in 2006 in a **massive X-ray machine**. This is **far hotter even than the Sun**, which burns at a mere **15 million °C (27 million °F).**

Get cracking

You can cook eggs in **Dominica's Boiling Lake**. The lake, in **Morne Trois Pitons National Park**, is part of a **volcano**. The **super-hot steam** that is forced through the **blue-grey water** makes it **bubble and spit** in the middle, **where it is deepest.**

Hot in the city

Although it doesn't get the **extreme temperatures** of some cities, **Thailand's capital, Bangkok,** is **the planet's hottest city** when judged by **year-round heat**. Temperatures are often **above 40°C (104°F) day and night**. The city's air is also **very polluted**, which helps **trap the heat in**, making it **even hotter!**

PLAYING WITH FIRE

Some people like to **fill their mouths with fuel** and blow it out in a **big stream of flame.** Others like to take **burning rods** and **put them out by swallowing the fire.** They are called **fire breathers and fire eaters**, and both of them can end up with a **blistery mouth** and a **burnt tongue. Ouch!**

I SHOULD NEVER HAVE HAD THAT CHILLI WITH BREAKFAST!

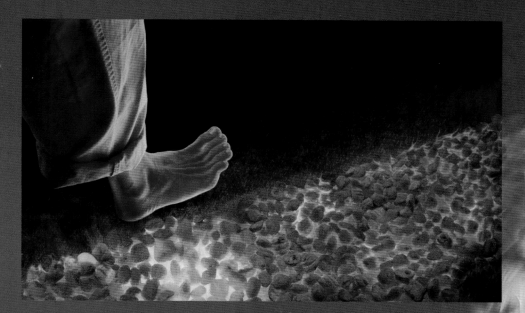

Hot footing it

On the **Fijian island of Beqa**, locals **walk barefoot over white-hot stones**. Legend says that the **islanders were given this power** over fire **by a spirit god**. In other parts of **Fiji, Indian Fijians also walk on hot coals**, during a **Hindu religious festival**.

Hot, hot, hot!

Death Valley, in California, is probably the consistently **hottest place on Earth**, with an **average summer temperature of 47°C (117°F)**. The **hottest air temperature** ever recorded was **57.8°C (136°F)** in **Al-Aziziyah, Libya**, in 1922. **Dasht-e Lut** in Libya is a **very dry and very hot desert plateau**. In some parts, nothing lives – **not even bacteria!**

Tongue blaster

The **hottest chilli in the world** is the **Trinidad Moruga Scorpion**. These **golf ball-size chillies** are about **240 times hotter than a jalapeño**. You should **wear gloves** and perhaps **even a mask** when cooking with these **fireballs**.

HOT STUFF

Cool facts about the hottest things

Warm welcome

The **Afar people** live in one of the **hottest** and **most inhospitable places** on Earth – the **Danakil Depression in Africa**. It is part of the **Great Rift, 120m (394ft) below sea level**, where **temperatures can reach 50°C (145°F)**. The earth is **cracked, lava oozes up** from below, and **tremors** regularly **shake the ground**. The Afar are **nomads**, herding **goats, camels and cattle**. They have also been described as one of the **fiercest tribes** on Earth.

WE HERDERS ROAM AFAR AND WIDE ...

These presidents really rock

Four giant heads are carved into the rocky cliffs of **Mt Rushmore** in the US state of **South Dakota**. The huge sculptures show **previous American presidents George Washington, Thomas Jefferson, Theodore Roosevelt** and **Abraham Lincoln**. Workers back in the **1920s** and **1930s** used **dynamite and jackhammers to carve** most of the features, and had to **hang off ropes** to do the work. **Each head** is about **18m (60ft) tall.**

> LOOK SHARP, GUYS – WE'RE ROCK LEGENDS!

TAKE A PEAK

Huge facts about the world's mighty mountains

Supreme forces at work

Mountains form when the **Earth's surface pushes, pulls, spews** and **folds**. Mountains are everywhere, **even under the water!** The **biggest mountains** form when huge pieces of the Earth, called **tectonic plates, push against each other** and then **fold upwards**. Some of the **rock at the top** of the **very highest mountains** actually formed at the **bottom of the ocean**, and was **pushed high into the sky**.

Equator

Feeling flat lately?

Did you know that the Earth is not perfectly round? Because **the world spins**, the two poles are **slightly flattened** and the **planet bulges a little bit at the equator**, just like a **beach ball** that someone is sitting on. **Mt Chimborazo**, in **Ecuador**, is **6268m (20,565ft) high** and very near the **equator**. That means its peak is **closer to the Moon** and **further from the centre of the Earth** than anywhere else on Earth.

16 seconds of terror

If you're **not keen on heights**, then you won't want to peer **over the edge** of **Mt Thor, in Canada**. It is famous for having the **world's longest purely vertical drop**. Leap off the top and you won't touch Earth again until you've fallen **1250m (4101ft)**. **(It will take about 16 seconds.)**

Great Atlantic secret

It's the **world's longest unbroken mountain chain**, but it wasn't known about until the **1920s**! **The Mid Atlantic Ridge** is a range of mountains in the **middle of the Atlantic Ocean**, about **10,000km (6200mi) long**. It has formed where **two tectonic plates** are **tearing the Earth apart**. Some of the mountains in the ridge **poke up above the sea** surface and have **formed islands**, including **Iceland** and **Bermuda**.

HEY, THIS ISN'T THE WAY TO THE CHAIRLIFT ...

Hiding its height

We all know **Mt Everest** in the **Himalayas** is the **world's tallest mountain, right?** **Maybe not!** Measured from **base to peak**, Hawaii's **Mauna Kea pips Mt Everest** by **1400m (4590ft)**. **Mauna Kea** is **10,200m (33,465ft)** tall, although **6000m (19,685ft) is beneath the ocean**. The peak of **Mt Everest**, at **8848m (29,029ft)**, is higher above sea level. And **Mt Everest is still growing** – by about **6mm (0.2in) every year**, because a **tectonic plate** beneath the **Himalayan mountain range** is being pushed up above another one. **Mt Everest** is also **moving sideways.**

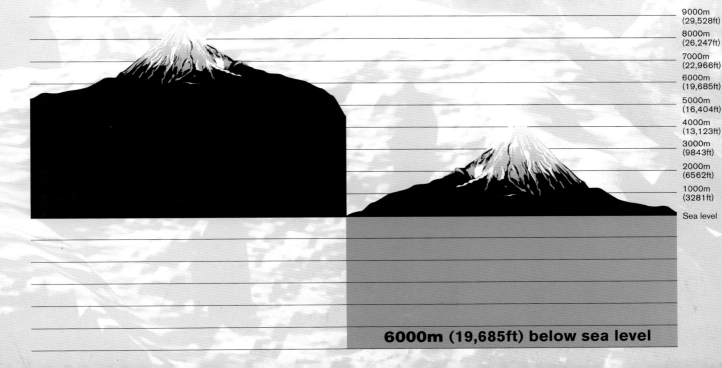

8848m (29,029ft)
Mt Everest

10,200m (33,465ft)
Mauna Kea

9000m (29,528ft)
8000m (26,247ft)
7000m (22,966ft)
6000m (19,685ft)
5000m (16,404ft)
4000m (13,123ft)
3000m (9843ft)
2000m (6562ft)
1000m (3281ft)
Sea level

6000m (19,685ft) below sea level

THOSE YAMS BETTER BE REALLY TASTY!

Fastest flying squirrel

Wingsuits are like special jumpsuits. Put one on and you can **fly like a bird**, or perhaps **a squirrel**, as they are also nicknamed **'flying squirrel suits'**. Jumping from a height of **9800m (32,000ft)**, a **Japanese wingsuit pilot** called **Shin Ito** set a few **new world records** in 2011: **the longest wingsuit flight** (23.1km/14.4mi), **the longest flight time** (5 minutes 22 seconds), and **the fastest speed** – an **incredible 363km/h** (226mph)!

Having a vine time

The **'land divers'** of **Pentecost Island** in **Vanuatu** were the **world's first bungee jumpers**. Every year, between April and June, young men **jump from tall wooden platforms**, with **vines tied to their ankles** to **stop them hitting the ground**. They sky-dive to show their **bravery** and **celebrate** the **yam crop**.

That's crazy!

Skydivers usually **jump from planes** with their **parachutes strapped to their backs**. But in **banzai skydiving** you **throw your parachute out of the plane**, then **leap out** after it, **freediving for a while** before trying to **catch it!**

I MUST HAVE BEEN NUTS TO TRY ON THIS SUIT

Rolling on

Invented in **New Zealand** in **1994**, a **zorb** is like a **hamster ball for kids**. You jump inside a **big plastic shock-absorbing ball** and **roll yourself down a grassy hill.**

Ride 'em cowboy

The **Calgary Stampede** in **Canada** is the **world's largest rodeo**, a **10-day long festival** held in July. There are **pancake breakfasts, barbecues** and even **chuckwagon racing**. More than **a million people** visit **'The Greatest Outdoor Show on Earth'** every year.

BORN TO BE WILD

Thrills and spills from around the world

Perfect gem

The blue **Logan Sapphire** is completely **flawless** and almost as **big as an egg**. It was found in Sri Lanka and is the **largest cut sapphire** on display in the world. It is set as a brooch, surrounded by **diamonds**. You can **see it** in the **Smithsonian Museum** of Natural History in the US.

BLUEST

The big blue yonder, in all its wonder

Claim to fame

The towns of **Chefchaouen**, in **Morocco**, and **Jodhpur**, in **India**, are both nicknamed '**the blue city**', as many of their buildings are painted a **beautiful** blue. Houses on the **Greek** island of **Santorini** are famous for their **domed blue roofs**.

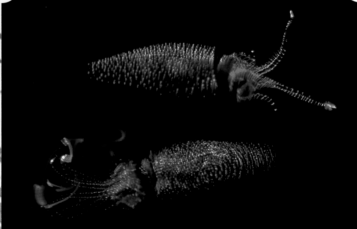

Squiddly diddly do

They are only 7.5cm (3in) long, but firefly squid in Japan's Toyama Bay can put on a **massive light show**. They have natural '**glowsticks**' all over their body that they can **flash on and off** to attract a mate and **confuse their enemies**. **Millions** of the flashy squid rise to the surface of the bay in May and June, turning the water **vibrant, writhing blue**.

Swallow that

Mighty blue whales are the **biggest animals** that have **ever lived on Earth**. They can grow up to **33m (110ft)** long, with a heart **the size of a small car**, and a tongue that weighs **2.7 tonnes (3 tons)**! But they could never swallow you up – their throats are so small, a **beach ball** wouldn't fit down there.

MY MIGHTY HEART IS WHAT DRIVES ME...

ANYTHING BLUE WILL DO!

Love nests

The **male bowerbirds** of New Guinea and Australia are **crazy** about blue. They build a beautiful nest, called a **bower**, on the ground, out of sticks and grass, then **decorate** it with all kinds of **funny** objects – especially blue ones! **Anything goes: feathers**, berries, **flowers**, bones, **fruit**, shells, bits of **plastic**, glass, a toothbrush or **glass eye** – as long as it looks **neat** and **pretty** for his special **lady** friend.

Funny furry friend

This creepy **greenbottle blue tarantula** crawls around the **deserts** of Venezuela, South America.

SCALING 7 SUMMITS

Imagine climbing to the **highest point on every continent**. You need **very strong legs and lungs** to **climb millions of steps**. The **first person** to do it was **Richard Bass**, in **1985**. So far, **only a few hundred people** have managed this feat.

1 Asia Mt Everest, Nepal **8848m (29,029ft) 2 South America** Aconcagua, Argentina **6962m (22,841ft) 3 North America** Denali, Alaska **6194m (20,320ft) 4 Africa** Mt Kilimanjaro, Tanzania **5895m (19,340ft) 5 Europe** Mt Elbrus, Russia **5642m (18,510ft) 6 Antarctica** Vinson Massif **4897m (16,067ft) 7 Oceania** Puncak Jaya (Mount Carstensz), Indonesia **4884m (16,024ft)**

DOGGONE IT... I'M IN THE WRONG RACE!

BRRRRRRRING IT ON!

Have you heard of the **Iditarod Trail Sled Dog Race** in **Alaska**? You can read all about it on **page 129**. Some people do **a solo version of the race**, called the **Iditarod Trail Invitational**. It is held in **winter**, and contestants have to **run, cycle or ski** through **blizzards and sub-zero temperatures** – without the help of **furry four-footed doggy friends**. You can't enter the full **1600km (1000mi) race** unless you have managed to finish an **'easy' 560km (350mi)** version first.

EXTREME ENDURANCE

Some of the toughest, longest, craziest challenges on Earth

ON YOUR BIKE!

3500km (approx)
Tour de France

FRENCH CONNECTION Imagine pedalling **3000–4000km (1800–2500mi)** over **21 days**. That's what **elite cyclists** from **all over the world do**, trying to win the **Tour de France**. The course is **a bit different every year**, and is staged over **set distances every day**, but the race always **winds over steep hills** and **mountains**, with **a few sprint races thrown in**, and ends in **Paris**. To complete the **European Grand Tour**, you would also have to finish the **long-distance Tour of Italy** and the **Tour of Spain** in the **same year**.

4800km (approx)
Race Across America

GREAT AMERICAN BIKE RACE Now imagine doing the **Tour de France in about 10 days**, rather than **spread out over 3 weeks**. Chances are you might be in the **transcontinental Race Across America**, from the **US west coast to the east coast**. The route is different every year, but you'll be going pretty much **non-stop** for about **4800km (3000mi)**. The first race in **1982** had only **four riders**.

12,000km (approx)
Tour d'Afrique

STAR OF AFRICA If you need **an even longer** bicycle race, try the **12,000km (7456mi) Tour d'Afrique race**, from **Cairo** to **Cape Town**. It starts in **Egypt in the north of Africa**, and ends at the **very southern tip of South Africa**.

Norses for courses

You have to be **as strong as a Viking** to finish the **Norseman triathlon** in **Norway**. First you have to **swim across a freezing cold lake**… then **bicycle 180km (112mi)** up into the **chilly hills**… and then **run a full 42km (26mi) marathon**, finishing **on top of a mountain**. Anyone who makes it to the end **gets a black t-shirt** for their troubles.

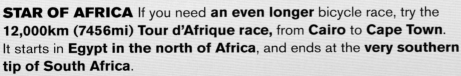

BUT I DON'T EVEN LIKE CARROTS!

What's big, red, cumbersome and the best-known symbol of London?

London's old red buses look top-heavy, but they can *lean at more than 40 degrees* and not tip over.

Flaming fowl

The **only red shorebird** in the **world**, the **scarlet ibis** lives on islands in the **Caribbean Sea** and parts of tropical **South America**. It is **not born red**, but starts out in life **greyish white**. It **gets its colour** from the **red shellfish it eats**, which contains **carotenoid** – the same **natural pigment as carrots** have. So it's true: **you are what you eat!**

Pretty deadly

Strawberry poison-dart frogs look good enough to eat – but you would **die if you did**. **South American hunters** use the **poison** from these tiny red frogs on their **hunting arrows**.

DANGER! DANGER! DON'T LICK ME OR YOU'LL DIE ...

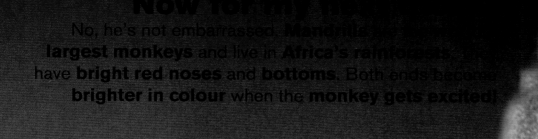

Now for my next...

No, he's not embarrassed. Mandrills are the world's **largest monkeys** and live in **Africa's rainforests.** They have **bright red noses** and **bottoms**. Both ends become **brighter in colour** when the **monkey gets excited!**

REDDEST

Colourful crimson-flushed curiosities

That's nuts

The **world's reddest teeth** belong to **betel nut eaters**. The betel nut is the **seed of a palm tree**. It is **chewed** by **people** in some parts of **Papua New Guinea, Southeast Asia** and the **Asia Pacific**.

How shellfish!

The **bright red giant Japanese spider crab** has the **largest leg span** of any **invertebrate – 3.8m (12ft)** from **claw to claw.** Imagine the **crab cake** you could make! **Pass the chilli sauce.**

Reddy to rock

Uluru is a **massive sandstone monolith** in the middle of **Australia**. It is **9.4km (5.8mi) round** and **350m (1148ft) high** – that's **higher** than the **Eiffel Tower**. It turns **bright red** at **sunrise** and **sunset**.

Elusive glittering prize

No wonder **gold costs so much**. Only **161,000 tonnes (177,000 tons)** of gold **has ever been mined**. It would all **fit in a room 17m (55ft) square**. Gold can be hammered into sheets so thin that a stack of **7000** of them would be only **as thick as a coin**. And **28g (1oz) of gold** could be **stretched out as a wire 80km (50mi) long!**

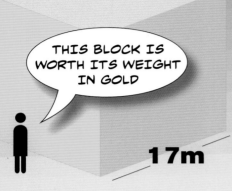

THIS BLOCK IS WORTH ITS WEIGHT IN GOLD

17m

That sinking feeling

All around the globe, there are thought to be some **3 million shipwrecks** sitting in **watery graves** beneath **the waves**.

Titanic discovery

In 1985, the **wreck of the Titanic** was discovered on the bottom of the **Atlantic Ocean**. The giant ocean liner hit an **iceberg and sunk** on its very first voyage from London to New York in **1912**, even though it was supposed to be **'unsinkable'**. Some of the items recovered from the wreck include **perfume bottles**, bottles of beer and wine, **a deck chair**, letters from passengers, **menus from the last meal served**, jewellery and clothes.

SECRETS FROM BELOW

Hidden treasures from beneath the earth and sea

Diamonds really are forever

If you go **diamond hunting**, look for a place where there have been **lots of volcanoes**. Most diamonds are formed **deep below the Earth's surface** under **huge pressures** and **high temperatures.** They are brought to the surface by **volcanic eruptions**. Many diamonds are almost as **old as the planet**. Some can be **more than 3 billion years old**.

Sea how they stand

Children stand silently in a **ring, holding hands**. But you'll need to put on a **swimming costume** and **wear goggles to see them**. They are part of an **underwater sculpture garden** at **Moliniere Bay, in Grenada**, that sits on the ocean floor **6.7m (22ft) below the surface**. The **65 figures** are casts of residents **who live in the nearby towns.**

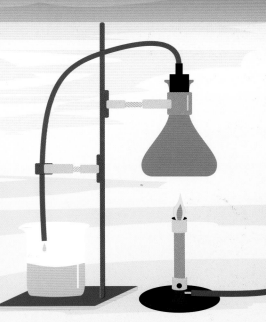

Get-rich scheme

If you want to **get rich**, work out a way of **getting gold out of sea water**. There are **18 million tonnes (20 million tons) of gold** in the **world's oceans**. It's just that **no one knows how to get to it yet!**

MY SCHOOL FLOATS!

In **Cambodia**, some **kids paddle to school**. They live in a **floating fishing village** called **Chong Khneas**, on **Tonlé Sap Lake**. They also have a small **floating basketball court** and a **floating church**. When they move their **houseboats**, they **tow their school** with them.

ZZZZ, MY THOUGHTS KEEP DRIFTING

A WHEELY GOOD SCHOOL

In **India**, some **mums and dads** who are very poor have to **move around a lot** looking for work. In **Goa**, a **'school on wheels'** follows their children around, so they can **still keep learning.**

OFF TO SCHOOL

Learning lessons from all around the world

Switched on

Imagine **sharing a school desk** with **someone** more than **1000km (620mi) away**. You'd probably be in the **world's biggest classroom**, in **outback Australia**. Its **eager pupils** are spread over **1.3 million sq km (nearly 502,000 sq mi)** – that's **five times bigger than the UK**, or **twice the size of Texas**. So **how do they get to school? They don't!** Teachers give them **lessons at home**, by **email**, **internet**, **video** and **phone**. These **'School of the Air' kids** used to **listen to their teacher over the radio,** and had to power their own radio by **pedalling it with their feet**. Now they get to **put their feet up**.

Take a big hike

Would you trudge 5 hours up a huge mountain to get to school? Some young kids in **China** do, to get to a faraway school in **Gulu village**. They go up a **very narrow path** cut into the **edge of the mountain**, with lots of **dangerous twists** that make them **dizzy**. They are not allowed to **throw balls** in case they **go over the cliff**. Most of these kids have **never seen a car or a computer.**

At school in **Japan,** kids have to **clean the school building for 10 minutes a day!** They wear **uniforms** and have special **rules** about **hairstyles, jewellery** and **make-up.**

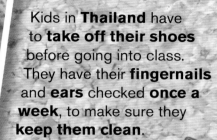

Kids in **Thailand** have to **take off their shoes** before going into class. They have their **fingernails** and **ears** checked **once a week,** to make sure they **keep them clean.**

In **African** countries like **Ghana, Malawi** and **Sudan,** some **classrooms are outdoors,** with desks set up **under trees.** If you go to school in **Zambia,** your school might have **walls and desks made of mud!**

Kids in **China** get **free school uniforms.** They go to school from **7.30am to 5pm,** with a **two-hour lunch break.** They do **eye exercises every day** – maybe because they use their **computers** so much.

Most kids in **France** don't go to school on **Wednesday;** instead they go to school for a **half-day on Saturday.** They go to school from **8am to 4pm,** and have a **two-hour lunch break.**

These boats never float

The **Henley-On-Todd Regatta** is one boat race where **you don't need to wear a life jacket**. That's because it takes place in a **dry riverbed** in **Alice Springs, Australia**. If there *is* water, the sailors would be in big trouble – **the boats have no bottom!** The boat crews race their boats by **picking them up while inside them** and **running to the finish line. Rain** is the **only thing that stops the regatta**, because the **river fills with water**.

WACKY SPORTS

Funny contests from around the globe

THE SUN'S VERY BRIGHT - BUT THOSE GUYS SURE AREN'T

Carrying on with the ladies

Every **July**, in **Sonkajarvi**, Finland, **burly men** throw a **lady over their shoulders**, then carry her over a **difficult obstacle course** in the **Wife Carrying World Championship**. The **couple who finish** in the **shortest time win** the **wife's weight in beer!**

Foot-brawl ups and downs

The **Royal Shrovetide Football** is a **huge moving brawl** that has been played for more than **1000 years** in the town of **Ashbourne**, in **England**. The **townspeople divide themselves** into two teams, the **Up'ards and Down'ards**, based on where they live, then try to carry a **leather ball** through the **hundreds-strong crowd** to **goalposts about 4.8km (3mi) apart** and **score**. There are very few rules, **but churchyards, cemeteries and private homes** are **out of bounds** – and you **can't murder your opponents**. It is believed the original ball was a **human head thrown to the crowd after an execution!**

WHERE ARE THE BRAKES ON THIS THING?

Going bananas

The **Tapati Rapa Nui Festival** on **Easter Island** features lots of **ancient Polynesian sports**, such as **sliding down a cliff** on a **banana tree**, **rowing across a lake** in a **reed raft** and **racing around the lake** carrying **bunches of bananas**. The festival is held in **January** and **February** and also features **feasts**, **music** and **dancing**.

Look, no hands...

In **Malaysia**, **Thailand** and **Indonesia**, people have been playing **sepak takraw**, or **kickball**, for **500 years**. It's a little like **volleyball** – except you **can't use** your **arms or hands**. You can **only use your feet, knees, head and chest** to get the ball **over the net**.

LIFE IN THE CITY

Fascinating facts about where most of us live

ALL PACKED IN

Almost **30,000** people live in **each square kilometre of Mumbai in India (77,700 people per sq mi)**, making it the **most densely populated city** on the **planet**. Per square kilometre, there are **10,200** people (26,400 per sq mi) in **New York**, **5100** people (13,200 per sq mi) in **London**, **3750** people (9700 per sq mi) in **Berlin** and **2100** people (5400 per sq mi) in **Sydney**.

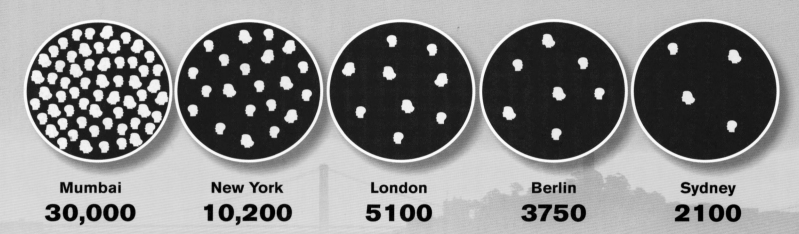

| **Mumbai** | **New York** | **London** | **Berlin** | **Sydney** |
| **30,000** | **10,200** | **5100** | **3750** | **2100** |

Middle East Manhattan

You might think **skyscrapers** are **very modern**, but in the **Middle East** people have been **building them** for **hundreds of years!** In **Yemen**, people in the town of **Shibam** live in **mud buildings** that **soar towards the heavens**. Some buildings are **11 storeys tall**. They were built this way to **protect locals** from **attacks** by desert people called **Bedouins**. The town is sometimes called the **'Manhattan of the desert'**.

Site for sore legs

You'll need a **good rest** after you've **walked up Baldwin Street** in the **New Zealand** city of **Dunedin**. It is the **world's steepest residential street**, which at its steepest **rises 1m (3.3ft) for every 3m (9.8ft)** you travel on it. Every year, **1000 runners** rush to the **top and back again** in the **Baldwin Street Gutbuster race**. An easier competition is the **Jaffa Race**, in which **30,000** of the orange lollies are **rolled down the hill** for charity.

HERE COME THE JAFFAS

Wait... wait... wait...

It can take a **long time** to cross the **12 lanes of traffic** on **9 de Julio Avenue** in **Buenos Aires, Argentina** – the **widest avenue in the world**. Usually pedestrians have to wait for **three changes of traffic lights** to make it **from one side to the other**. The road, which is **100m (328ft) wide**, spans **an entire city block**.

573 litres
(151 gallons)

How much water each person in the US uses each day.

10 litres
(3 gallons)

How much water each person in Ethiopia, Africa, uses each day.

Twisty tale

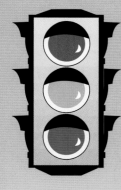

Every **Easter Sunday**, dozens of people **race tricycles** down Lombard Street in **San Francisco**. Most of them **fall off before they reach the bottom**, because it is **the crookedest street on Earth**. **Thousands of tourists** wander around its **eight really sharp** and **really steep corners every day**, probably dreaming of **racing a trike down it**. It has featured in lots of **movies** and **television shows**.

TOP 10 DIRTY CITIES

Cities can be **dirty, polluted places** with **air that can harm you**. The **10 cities** with the **worst air pollution**, according to the **World Health Organization**, are:

1 **Ahvaz**, Iran
2 **Ulaan Baatar**, Mongolia
3 **Sanandaj**, Iran
4 **Ludhiana**, India
5 **Quetta**, Pakistan
6 **Kermanshah**, Iran
7 **Peshawar**, Pakistan
8 **Gaborone**, Botswana
9 **Yasouj**, Iran
10 **Kanpur**, India

Stamp of a multi-millionaire

If you see this **tiny old stamp**, don't throw it away – it is worth almost **US$2.5 million**, enough to buy **100 family cars** and **build a garage big enough to put them all in!** Called the **Treskilling Yellow**, it is the **world's most valuable stamp** because it is the only **one of its kind**. It was made in **Sweden** in **1855**. It was **meant to be blue**, but somehow it was **printed yellow**.

Super-powered sunbeams

Every year, the **yellow Sun** in our sky sends down **20,000 times more energy** than **people use**. If we could **convert more of it into electricity**, then we **wouldn't need to burn oil, coal or gas** – and our **air** would be **so much cleaner**.

YELLOWEST

Gorgeous glittery golden gifts from round the globe

I SPY... A BOOTYLICIOUS GOLDEN FLY!

What's up doc?

If you **ate enough carrots**, your **skin would turn yellow**. That's because carrots **contain carotene**, which is a **pigment** that **gives carrots** their **colour**. You could **end up being** the **yellowest person** on the planet!

Flight of fancy

Scientists in Canberra, **Australia**, have named a **very rare horsefly** after the pop singer **Beyonce**, because it has a **shapely golden bottom**. The fly is officially called **Scaptia (Plinthina) beyonceae**.

Big yellow taxis

If you are in a **yellow taxi cab**, you are probably in **New York**. This great city has around **13,000 taxis**. Some **240 million passengers** make about **170 million trips** in them **every year**. The average New York taxi travels **130,000km (81,788mi) each year** – equal to **3.25 times around the world**. Before you are allowed to drive one, you have to go to **taxi school**.

ROUND AND ROUND THE WORLD I GO

Bet you didn't know
Insects have **yellow** blood!

IT'S SSSOO NICE TO SSSEE YOU...

S-s-s-wampy s-s-surpri-s-se

Yellow anacondas have **leopard-like markings**. They **lurk** around swamps in **South America** and **squeeze their prey to death** before **swallowing** it **whole**. Lucky for us they are much **smaller** than their big **green cousins** – they grow to about **3m (9.8ft)**; green ones can get almost **three times** as long.

Greatest gold digger
The **Grasberg Mine**, in the **Indonesian province of Papua**, is the **largest gold mine in the world** – a hole in the ground about **4km (2.5mi) wide**. It is located **high up in the mountains,** near an icy glacier.

Eyeball this sparkly gem
The world's **most expensive yellow diamond** sold for **US$10.9 million** in 2011. Called the **Sun-Drop Diamond**, it is the **largest yellow diamond on Earth**. It is as **big as an eyeball**.

EXTREME OCEAN

Our big blue planet is one mighty puddle!

Scariest waves around

Imagine screaming down a wave **as big as a 10-storey building** on a surfboard, with nothing but **rocks and coral** beneath you. **Big wave surfing** is one of the **most dangerous sports in the world**. Riders are **towed out to sea** by jetskis, before they **tackle waves** up to **27m (90ft) high!** Some of the **best big waves** can be found off **Australia**, **Hawaii**, **California** and **Portugal**.

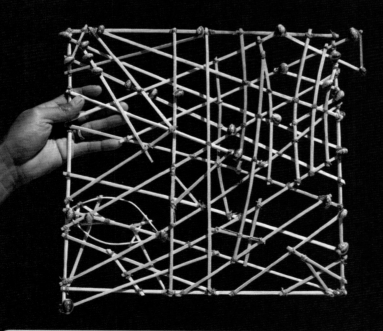

...AND THERE ARE NO NOSY NEIGHBOURS!

Long way from home

Bouvet is the **most remote island in the world**. You'll find it in the **South Atlantic Ocean**, 2525km (1570mi) southwest of South Africa (about a **two-week sail** in a yacht, if you're lucky). It is **covered in ice**, and only **moss, seals, birds** and **penguins** live there. In **1979**, a satellite recorded a **flash of light not far from Bouvet Island**, which scientists think might have been caused by a **nuclear explosion**, or a **meteor striking the Earth**.

Sticking with it

People from the **Marshall Islands**, way out in the middle of the vast **Pacific Ocean**, used **stick charts** to **navigate their canoes** between islands. The stick charts were like modern maps, **showing islands**, **wind directions** and **ocean currents**.

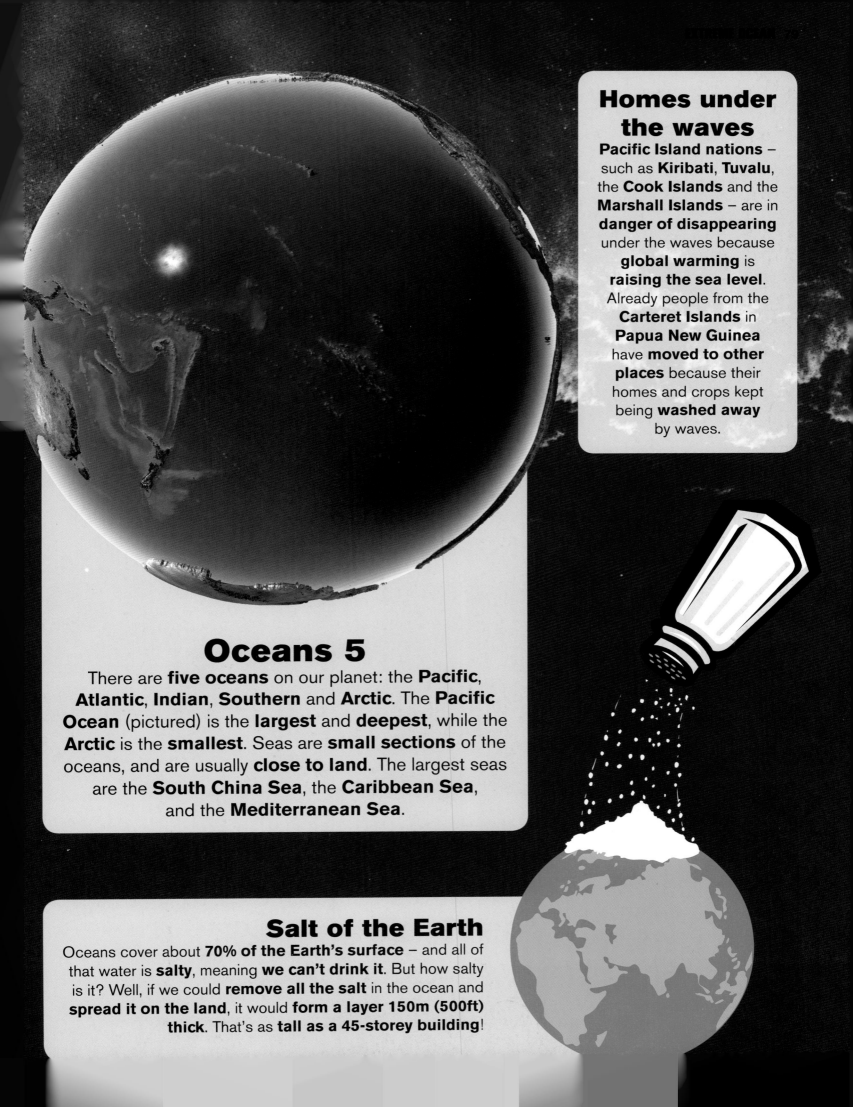

Homes under the waves

Pacific Island nations – such as **Kiribati**, **Tuvalu**, the **Cook Islands** and the **Marshall Islands** – are in **danger of disappearing** under the waves because **global warming** is **raising the sea level**. Already people from the **Carteret Islands** in **Papua New Guinea** have **moved to other places** because their homes and crops kept being **washed away** by waves.

Oceans 5

There are **five oceans** on our planet: the **Pacific, Atlantic, Indian, Southern** and **Arctic**. The **Pacific Ocean** (pictured) is the **largest** and **deepest**, while the **Arctic** is the **smallest**. Seas are **small sections** of the oceans, and are usually **close to land**. The largest seas are the **South China Sea**, the **Caribbean Sea**, and the **Mediterranean Sea**.

Salt of the Earth

Oceans cover about **70% of the Earth's surface** – and all of that water is **salty**, meaning **we can't drink it**. But how salty is it? Well, if we could **remove all the salt** in the ocean and **spread it on the land**, it would **form a layer 150m (500ft) thick**. That's as **tall as a 45-storey building**!

Rails across Russia

It takes **seven days** to travel right along **the world's most famous continuous long-distance railway: the 9289km (5772mi) Trans–Siberian railway**, across Russia. **It crosses seven time zones** and stretches from **Moscow** in the west, to **Vladivostok** in the east. That's about **the same distance** as travelling from **London, England** to **Tokyo, Japan**.

MOSCOW

VLADIVOSTOK

Distance	1000km	2000km	3000km	4000km	5000km	6000km	7000km	8000km	9289km
Typical Transit times	0D13H35M	1D3H55M	1D14H10M	2D4H25M	2D17H10M	4D2H45M	4D17H15M	6D1H55M	6D18H13M

ON THE RAILS

Some wheely interesting facts about railways

Model magic

Miniatur Wunderland, in **Hamburg, Germany**, recreates **Europe and the US** on a **small scale**. But it is still **large enough** to be the **biggest model railway** in the world. It has enough **little figures of people** to **populate a large city**, and the track is **9km (6mi) long**.

What a mouthful

The **very small railway station** in the **small village** of **Llanfairpwllgwyngyll**, in Wales, has the **longest railway station name** in the world:

LLANFAIRPWLLGWYNGYLLGOGERYCHWYRNDROBWLLLLANTYSILIOGOGOGOCH

Llan-vire-pooll-guin-gill-go-ger-u-queern-drob-ooll-llandus-ilio-gogo-goch

ARRIVA

It means **'Saint Mary's Church** in a **hollow of white hazel** near the **swirling whirlpool** of the **church of Saint Tysilio** with a **red cave'.** Huh?

HEY, LET ME OUT – THIS IS MY STOP!

WHY DID WE SAY WE'D MEET IN THE LAST CAR?

Oresome ride

Lots of people like to travel on the **world's longest train**, but most of them don't sit in seats. The **3km (1.9mi) long train**, in the **African** country of **Mauritania**, carries **iron ore**. People like to catch a **free ride on top** of one of its **200 or so** carriages.

Pushy people

Tokyo's subway system is **so busy** it employs people called **oshiyas** to **push people into the trains** so the **doors can close!** Passengers make more than **3 billion trips** on the world's **busiest subway system** every year.

Look, no wheeeeels!

In **Japan** they have trains that **float on magnets** and can **go very fast**. One train travelled at **581km/h (361mph)** – almost **half the speed of sound**.

Angriest ant ordeal

People say being **stung by a bullet ant** is like being **shot with a gun**. Bullet ants have the **most painful sting** of any **insect on Earth**! So imagine slipping on some **gloves filled with dozens** of these **angry, stinging ants**. That's what **boys** from the **Satere-Mawe** tribe in **Brazil** have to do during the **world's most painful** initiation ceremony. They have to **wear the gloves** for **10 minutes** and **try not to shout or scream** as the ants keep stinging them. Their **arms** are often **temporarily paralysed** from the **ant venom**, and they may **shake for days**. The boys have to **endure this ritual 20 times!**

IT'S THE PURRFECT DISGUISE...

I'M A GUN AT MAKING BOYS SCREAM!

Twitchy whiskers

The **Matsés** people, who live in the **Amazon**, make themselves **look like jaguars** by getting **special tattoos** on their faces, and **inserting palm tree splinters** through their **nose or cheeks**, to look like **cat's whiskers**.

Making their mark

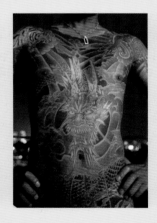

New Zealand's Maori people use **small chisels** to **carve grooves** into their skin. These **tribal tattoos** are called **ta moko**. **Important** people often had a **ta moko** pattern **on their face,** so everyone could see **how important** they were.

Japanese gangsters called **Yakuza** often sport **amazingly intricate full-body tattoos** to show other people they are **part of a gang**.

People in the **Chin Hills** of **Myanmar** use **tattoos** to distinguish **one hill tribe** from another. Many **young girls** have their **faces tattooed**.

Some **Samoan** men get a **pe'a body tattoo**, from their **waist** to their **knees**. It takes **many weeks** to complete and is **very painful**. **Samoan women** sometimes have a **malu tattoo** on their **legs**, from below the **knee** to the **upper thigh**.

Inuit girls used to **tattoo their faces** as a sign of **strength and beauty**. They would dip **animal tendons** in **black ink**, then **thread** the tendons **through their faces** to leave the **ink stains behind**.

Hanging around

Every **Good Friday**, villagers in the **northern Philippines** provinces of **Pampanga** and **Bulacan** recreate the **crucifixion** of **Jesus Christ** by having themselves **nailed to crosses** and then **tortured**. **Thousands of people** come to watch the ceremony.

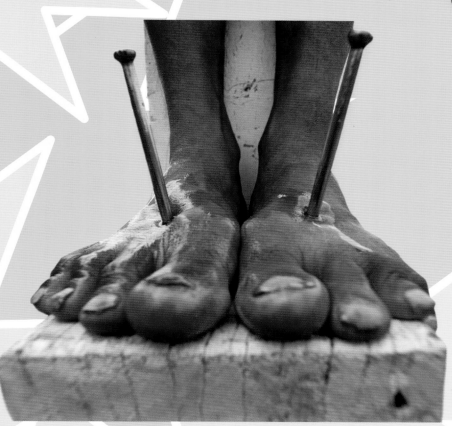

THAT'S GOTTA HURT!

Some of the ouchiest things on the planet

Don't be cheeky!

At the **nine-day Phuket Vegetarian Festival** in **Thailand**, men and women go **into a trance**, then **stick knives, skewers** or other **sharp objects** through their **cheeks, tongues** and other body bits, or **run across burning-hot coals** in **bare feet!** Definitely **not something** you should try at home.

SURELY THERE'S A BETTER WAY TO PLAY THE GUITAR

Playing with rays

The **huge stingrays** at **Stingray City** on the **Cayman islands** in the **Caribbean** are so tame they will **come right up to you**. They don't actually **'sting'**, but they do have a **pointy barb** under their tail that they **use for protection**.

ALL MY FRIENDS JUST CALL ME RAY...

Tetra packs it in

Blind Mexican tetra fish that live in caves **used to have eyes**, but because they have spent the last **million or so years in the dark**, their skin has **grown over their peepers**. Mysteriously, they **avoid bumping into** other fish. No-one really **understands** why.

Tiny fish in a tiny puddle

The **world's smallest fish** is also the **world's smallest animal with a backbone**. The tiny **see-through carp** is only **8mm (0.3in) long** and lives in **swamps** in **Sumatra** and **Borneo**. It **doesn't mind a drought** because it can **live** in the **tiniest puddles**. These fish are **so small** you could hide one **under your fingernail!**

I thought you were dead!

Everyone thought the **coelacanth fish** had died out **65 million years ago**, until a **live one turned up** off the coast of **South Africa** in **1938**! The fish has been around since **before dinosaurs roamed the Earth**.

Big fish in a big pond

The **biggest fish in the world** could **swallow you** in one gulp! **Whale sharks** can grow almost **13m (42ft) long**, but they would **never dream of eating you** – they like food that is much smaller. They are **very calm** creatures, **cruising slowly** around the warm oceans. Divers sometimes **hitch a ride** on the back of one.

Long life down under

If you were a fish and you wanted to **live a long life**, you would head to **the bottom** of the **darkest, deepest oceans**. Down there, **fish live longer** than we do. Some **rockfish**, living about **3000m (9800ft) below** the ocean surface, are more than **200 years old!** Most of them live in the Pacific Ocean.

FISHY BUSINESS

Funny facts about our finny friends

I BET THEY'RE ALL GREEN WITH ENVY!

Flashy splashy

Lake Malawi in Africa contains **more fish species** than **any other lake** on Earth – including more than **300 different types** of these **colourful cichlid fish**.

WONDER IF THE SNACK BAR SELLS HOT CHIPS?

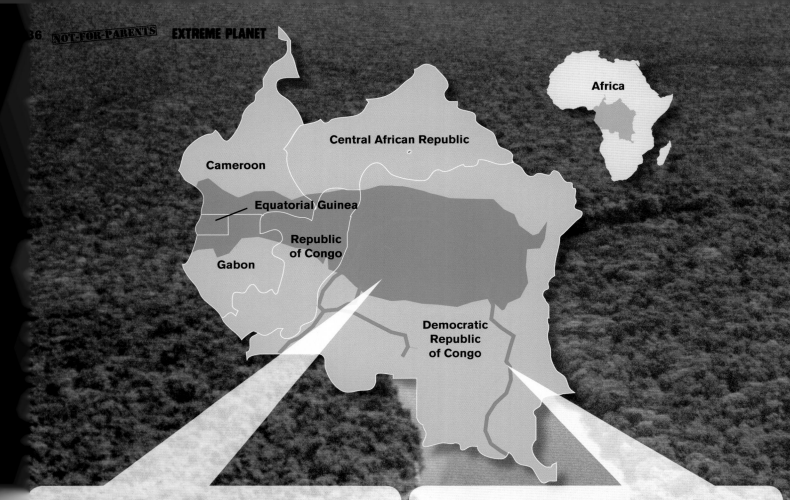

Congo Rainforest

- **World's second biggest rainforest**, after the Amazon.
- Home to **11,000 plant** species, **1150 bird** species, **450 mammal** species, **300 reptile** species and **200 amphibian** species.
- In some parts, the forest is **so thick** that the **only way** to travel through it is **by boat**, along the Congo River – and **modern explorers** haven't been able to get in there.
- Each year, more forest is being **chopped down** because of **logging**, **mining** and to **make room** for **crops and villages**.
- Many forest animals – **like gorillas** – are being **killed and eaten** by hungry people as **'bush meat'**.

Congo River

- **Home to** almost **700 fish** species.
- **World's deepest river:** some stretches are over **195m (640ft) deep**.
- By volume of water, it is **Africa's largest river** – even though it is not as long as **Africa's longest river,** the **Nile**. (The **Congo** is **4700km**/2900mi, the **Nile** is **6650km**/4130mi.)
- It **crosses the equator twice**, and in some parts is up to **24km** (15mi) **wide**.
- Its **falls** and **rapids** have **as much power** as **all the rivers and falls in the US** put together. Some rapids are so **fast and powerful** they are **too dangerous to cross** – such as the **120km** (75mi) long **'Gates of Hell'**.

CONGO CRAZY

Africa's biggest rainforest and river are home to some amazing people, plants and animals

Forest people

Many native people live in **small traditional tribes** in the forest, including the **Mbuti** and **Mbenga people**. They are **very short** – some of the men **grow less than 150cm** (4ft 11in) **tall**. They **hunt and gather** their food from the forest, making a **new camp** in another part of the forest when **food runs low**. Their **way of life** is **in danger** because other people are **chopping their forest down**.

Deadly work

Would you climb **30m** (100ft) **up a tree**, using **just your legs**, to gather honey from a hive full of **angry bees?** The **very bravest** Mbuti men do, because their tribe **loves honey**. A bird called the **greater honeyguide** shows them where the **beehives are**.

WHO SPLASHED THAT PAINT ALL OVER ME?

Animals found only here

What has a **brown body** like a **horse**, **legs** like a **zebra**, **a tongue** like a **giraffe** – and is found **nowhere else on Earth?** Why, the **okapi** of course! It is a **close cousin** of the giraffe – the males even have short, **hair-covered horns** like giraffes. Okapi are **hard to spot** in the forest as their **crazy colouring** gives them **excellent forest camouflage**.

THOSE HUMAN COUSINS LOOK PRETTY KOOKY TO ME...

Peace-loving **bonobo apes** are **our closest relatives**, sharing over **98% of our DNA**. In **bonobo land**, it is the **ladies** who are **top boss**.

The **elusive Congo peacock** is **hard** to spot.

Nuts about bird banks

Woodpeckers **peck holes** in trees and **hide acorns** in them so they have **something to eat** when the weather **turns nasty**. Some trees where they **store their nuts** have more than **50,000 holes** in them!

Great crater creator

In the past, **meteors** from **outer space** have **hit the Earth**, leaving **great big holes** in the ground. The **Vredefort crater**, in South Africa, is the **largest one ever**. It is **300km** (190mi) **wide** and was probably caused by a **meteor 5–10km** (3.1–6.2mi) across. It is thought a meteor hitting the Earth **many millions of years ago** may have **wiped out the dinosaurs**.

What a gas

A **Swiss cheese** called **Emmental** has **holes all through it,** because when it is made **gas** gets **caught inside**, causing **great big bubbles**. Emmental is Switzerland's **oldest cheese**.

Fine mine is an all-round wonder

Bingham's **Canyon Mine**, in the US state of **Utah**, is the **world's largest human-made hole** in the ground. It is more than **1.2km** (0.75mi) **deep** and **4km** (2.5mi) **wide**. **Twelve aircraft carriers** would **fit end to end** across the top of the mine, and **three Empire State Buildings** could sit **one on top of the other** and only just reach the rim. More than **408,000 tonnes** (450,000 tons) **of rock, dirt and minerals** are taken out of the mine **every day**.

Down the sink

In 2010, a **massive hole** opened up in the middle of **Guatemala City** in Guatemala. The hole was **18m** (60ft) **wide** and **100m** (300ft) **deep**. It was probably caused by **heavy rain** and a **leaky sewer pipe**. Sinkholes can suddenly form when **rocks and soil** beneath the surface are **washed away** by water. You **never know** when the earth is going to **open up beneath you!**

HOLEY MOLEY!

The hole truth about the holey-est things around

Girls giving lip

Mursi girls in **Ethiopia** make **huge holes** in their **lips** and **earlobes** by sticking **big clay plates** in them. It shows they are **becoming an adult**.

IT COSTS ME A FORTUNE TO BUY LIPSTICK!

Digging deep

In **1970**, **Russia** started **drilling a hole** in the ground just to **see what was down there**. They stopped in **1989** when they got down to **12,262m** (40,230ft), making it the **deepest hole ever drilled** into the surface of the Earth. What they found was that it is **extremely hot** down there – **180°C** (356°F) – and that there is **lots of water** and **hydrogen gas**.

NOISIEST

Some things make the biggest racket!

The key to quiet

The **quietest piece of music** is **John Cage's 4'33"**. It consists of the pianist **sitting at the piano** and **not hitting any keys** for 4 minutes and 33 seconds! Cage wrote another piece of music, **Organ²/ASLSP (As SLow aS Possible)**, that is **currently being played** in Germany. You've got **plenty of time** to catch it: the recital **won't end until 2640**.

WOW, THIS LEEK IS REALLY OUT OF TUNE...

Singing willie in training

The **loudest animal for its size** is the water boatman, a **tiny insect** about the size of the **head of a drawing pin** that makes its big noise by **rubbing its tiny willie** against its belly, to 'sing'! It makes **as much noise** as a passing **subway train**.

World's loudest vegetables

If you like **playing with your food**, maybe you could join the **Vienna Vegetable Orchestra** in Austria. The musicians play instruments **carved out of vegetables!** You might hear **carrot flutes** or **recorders**, **celery guitars**, **cucumber trumpets**, **eggplant cymbals**, **pumpkin drums**, **leek violins** and a **gurkaphon** (a hollowed-out cucumber). They use up to **70kg** (150lb) of **fresh vegetables** for each concert. After the show, the audience gets to **eat a soup** made from the **vegetables**!

Little shrimp is a real stunner

Pistol shrimps **stun** and **sometimes kill** their dinner just **by making a noise**! They are the **loudest animal in the world.** They make bubbles by **snapping their claws together**, and when the **bubbles pop** it makes the most **frightful noise.** Whole colonies of shrimp are **loud enough** to keep seaside towns **awake at night!**

IT'S LIKE TEXTING, ONLY LOUDER!

The hills are alive ...

Yodellers and **horn blowers** flock to **Switzerland** every **three years** for the **Swiss Yodelling Festival. Yodelling** is like a type of **loud singing** that **animal herders** in the **Alps** once used to **talk to each other** across the valleys.

Lowdown on London

London must be one of the **loudest cities around**. There are more than **32,000 musical performances** in London **every year** – that's **620** a week! **Quite a racket!**

World's 5 BIGGEST lakes

394,300 sq km
(152,240 sq mi)
Caspian Sea – Russia, Azerbaijan, Kazakhstan, Turkmenistan, Iran

82,400 sq km
(31,800 sq mi)
Lake Superior – Canada, US

69,485 sq km
(26,830 sq mi)
Lake Victoria – Tanzania, Uganda

59,600 sq km
(23,000 sq mi)
Lake Huron – Canada, US

58,000 sq km
(22,400 sq mi)
Lake Michigan – US

The **Caspian Sea** is **considered a lake** because it is **enclosed all around by land.** The **next four largest** lakes would **easily fit** inside it – **as well as** the **next four largest** after that: **Lake Aral** (Kazakhstan, Uzbekistan), **Lake Tanganyika** (Tanzania, Congo), **Lake Baikal** (Russia) and **Great Bear** (Canada).

Monster tales

Since ancient times, people around the world **have been seeing** different kinds of **lake monsters** – from the **black, serpent-like Pinatubo** of the Philippines, the **ogopogo** of Canada, the **mysterious mokèlé-mbèmbé** and the **emela-ntouka** of Africa, to the **bunyips** of outback Australia. The **most famous** is Scotland's **Loch Ness Monster**, nicknamed '**Nessie**'. Do such creatures really exist? The **only way to find out** is to **look for them yourself...**

AM I JUST A FIGMENT OF MY IMAGINATION?

So who's counting?

Finland in **northern Europe** is called the '**Land of a thousand lakes**'. Actually, it has **187,888 lakes!** But **that's nothing** compared to **Canada**, which has **so many lakes**, both **huge and small**, that **no one** has been able to **count them all!** Canada has **31,752 lakes** with an area of at least **3 sq km** (1.16 sq mi) – but there are **countless more** smaller lakes ... as well as some really huge lakes: **14** of them **bigger than 10,000 sq km** (3861 sq mi)!

Russian record-breaker

The **world's largest, deepest** and **oldest freshwater lake** is Lake Baikal in Siberia. It holds **20%** of the **planet's fresh water**. In winter, it **freezes** into a **great big ice-block**.

LOTS OF LOVELY LAKES

Planet Earth has over 304 million lakes – that's a splashy amount of water!

Pass the pepper please...

The **world's largest dried salt lake** is Salar de Uyuni, high up in the **Andes Mountains** in Bolivia (pictured). It covers **10,582 sq km** (4086 sq mi), and the **salt** in some parts is over **10m** (33ft) **thick**. When it rains, the lake is **covered in water** and becomes the **world's largest** natural mirror! **Pink flamingos** breed here.

GULP, THERE'S NO PLACE LIKE GNOME!

Psst, can you keep a SECRET?

Wast Water, in the **UK**, has a **secret 'gnome garden'** at the bottom of it. In **2005, police removed** the gnomes because they were planted very deep and **some divers died** trying to find them – but other divers keep **putting more gnomes back** in the lake. They are surely the **world's wettest** and **deepest-dwelling gnomes**! Divers say there are about **40 gnomes, and growing**. One gnome is nicknamed **Gordon**, another is **wearing a scuba diving outfit**, there is a **gnome with a lawnmower**, and a **gnome sitting on a wooden aeroplane**. There is even a **Christmas tree** down there!

Great Scot, what'll they do next?

The **Scottish** don't mind **throwing the odd strange thing**. In fact they have a **whole competition** full of it. The **Highland Games** is like a Scottish version of the **Olympic Games**. **Caber tossing** is like **throwing a huge telegraph pole**; in the **sheaf toss**, they **throw a bundle of wheat** over a bar. Contestants can also **hurl a haggis** – the **sausage-type Scottish treat** made from **boiled sheep's heart, lungs** and **liver**.

THIS TOSS WILL PUT ME IN 'POLE POSITION'

CRAZY CONTESTS

Champions do the strangest things

Greatest gobblers

You have to be **at least 18 years old** before you can enter **Major League Eating** contests. The idea is to **wolf down** as **much food** as you can in a **set time** – usually a **matter of minutes**. Contestants like to think they're **sports champions**! Past records include eating **68 hotdogs** in 10 minutes, **47 pizza slices** in 10 minutes, **49 glazed doughnuts** in 8 minutes and **3.8kg** (8.4lb) of **baked beans** in 2 minutes 47 seconds. First held in the US, events are now staged **around the world**.

Pressed for excitement

It could be the **tidiest sport around**, if not the **most exciting**. People participating in **Extreme Ironing** take an **ironing board** to a **remote location** and **iron clothes**. Clothes have been ironed while **parachuting**, **scuba diving**, **mountain climbing**, **skiing** and **canoeing**.

LOOK AT ME –
NO STRINGS
ATTACHED!

Up in the air

Do you ever **pretend to play the guitar** when you hear a **song you love**? Of course you do. Some people in **Finland** liked doing it **so much** they started a competition. The **Air Guitar World Championship** is held in the town of **Oulu** and attracts **dozens of contestants** and **thousands** of devoted fans.

Beat without beating

Capoeira is a **Brazilian game** that combines **martial arts**, **music** and **dancing**. People **stand in a circle**, musicians **provide the beat** and two people in the middle **jump**, **turn**, **strike** and **kick at each other**, usually **without connecting**. The idea is to **show skill** rather than **hurt someone**.

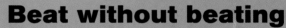

Check mate ouch!

One of the **strangest sports around** must be **chess boxing**. Two contestants **play a match** lasting **11 rounds**. In each round they **play 4 minutes of chess**, and then **box against each other for 2 minutes**.

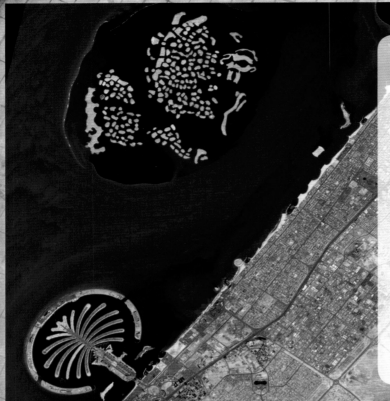

Unreal islands

The **Middle Eastern** desert country of **Dubai** is home to the **largest artificial islands in the world**. The **'Palm Islands'** are built in the **shape of palm trees**, from **sand dredged from the bottom** of the ocean, and are about **5km** (3mi) **across**. In Dubai they are also building a **group of islands** called **'The World'**, which will look like a **map of the world** when **viewed from space**.

I'M SAFE FOR A WHILE IF THE SEA LEVEL RISES

Small and light

The **smallest island** in the world is **Bishop Rock**, off the **UK coast**. It is only about **46m** (151ft) **long** and **16m** (52ft) **wide** and is almost **completely covered by a lighthouse**. Many years ago **criminals** were **sent to the island to die**.

Hot and spicy

The **Maluku** and **Banda** islands in **Indonesia** are the **spiciest islands in the world**. They were once called the **Spice Islands** because **rare spices** such as **nutmeg**, **mace** and **cloves** grew there. Banda was once the **only place in the world** where **nutmeg grew**. In the **1600s** nutmeg was **more valuable than gold**!

Far, far away

If you want to really get **away from it all**, try **Tristan da Cunha**, in the southern Atlantic Ocean. The island is **2816km** (1750mi) from anywhere else, making it the **most remote inhabited island** in the world. There's one radio station and **262 people** on the island.

THIS ISLAND IS FULL OF CRAZY QUACKS LIKE ME!

TREASURE ISLANDS

Ahoy there! I spy sanctuaries in the sea

The land that time forgot

The **Galápagos Islands**, in the **Pacific Ocean** off the coast of **South America**, are a **most unusual** spot. Almost **9000 different species of animals** live here. Because they have been **isolated from the mainland** for **so many millions of years**, many of the animals are found **nowhere else in the world** – such as **giant tortoises**, **marine iguanas** and the **Galápagos penguin** – the only penguin that lives on the equator.

RESERVE BANK OF ZIMBABWE
100 000 000 000 000
ONE HUNDRED TRILLION DOLLARS
AA0777821

Who wants to be a trillionaire?

It's **easy to be a trillionaire** if you live in **Zimbabwe**. In **2009**, the African country introduced the world's **biggest recent banknote**: a 100 trillion dollar note. **How much is 1 trillion?** Answer: it is **1 million million**. But something **doesn't add up**, because the **100 trillion dollar** note is **only worth about US$300!**

Funny money

If you go to **Disneyland**, you can use **Disney dollars**. Issued in **1987**, they come in **$1, $5** and **$10 notes**, and are the **same value** as the **US dollar**.

DISNEY DOLLARS
ONE DISNEY DOLLAR

SZÁZMILLIÓ B-PENGŐ
BUDAPEST, 1946. ÉVI JÚNIUS HÓ 3-ÁN
MAGYAR NEMZETI BANK

Lot of zeros make little cents

The **highest banknote ever** was the **100 million billion pengo**, issued in **Hungary** in **1946**. That's **100,000,000,000,000,000 pengos**. It was **only worth** about **20 US cents**.

BIG BUCKS

Money makes the world go round – but it's not all dollars and sense

BRING A CHISEL IF YOU WANT SMALL CHANGE

Mega money

When you want to **buy anything** on the island of **Yap** in **Micronesia**, you have to come up with **big money**. Make that **HUGE money**. Some of the island's currency is made from **stone discs**, up to **4m** (13ft) **across** and weighing up to **7.3 tonnes** (8 tons) called **rai stones**. Luckily the islanders know **who owns each piece**, so they can **leave them in one spot**.

Things that have been used as money

Before **coins** and **paper notes** were invented, people used **all sorts of things** as currency.
Many of the items they **traded** were **valued** because they were **useful, rare or beautiful**.
Below are **just some** of the items **people once used** as money **around the world**.

BEADS

PRECIOUS GEMS

SALT
(where the word 'salary' comes from)

BUTTER

PRECIOUS METALS

SHELLS
(where the phrase 'shelling out' comes from)

CAMELS

GRAIN

SNAILS

CHEESE

PEARLS

TEA LEAVES

COWS

RATS

The **outer layer** of our Earth is called **the crust**. But it's not **one whole piece**. Instead it's made up of **lots of smaller pieces**, like a **jigsaw puzzle**. And all those separate pieces, called **tectonic plates**, are **constantly moving** and **bumping against** each other. Earthquakes occur when **two of these plates** that are touching **suddenly move**. The power of an earthquake is called its **magnitude**, and is **measured out of 10**. **Volcanoes** are also **often found** around the **edges of tectonic plates**, where the Earth's crust is thinner.

SHAKY PLANET

Solid earth isn't always as solid as we think

Shaking all over

About **1.5 million earthquakes shake the world** each year. That is almost **three earthquakes every minute**! Thankfully, most are **so small** you **can't feel them**.

Hi there neighbour!

In the US state of **California**, the **Pacific** and **North American tectonic plates** on the **San Andreas Fault** are sliding past each other at **56mm** (2in) **every year** – about as **fast as your fingernails grow**. The city of **Los Angeles** is on one plate, and the city of **San Francisco** is on the other. Even though they are now **560km (348mi) apart**, they'll **slide past** each other in about **15 million years**.

Hell's furnace

If you could fly over **Nyiragongo volcano** in the **Democratic Republic of Congo**, Africa, and **look into its crater**, you would see an **amazing light show**. The brilliant show is caused by the **most violent molten lava lake** in the world that **spits** and **bubbles** and **glows bright orange**. The lava is coming from **deep under the Earth**.

Nature's raw explosive power

The **Pacific Ring of Fire** is the **world's most volcanic area**. It is a **40,000km** (25,000mi) **horseshoe** of **452 volcanoes** and **constant earthquakes**, around the edges of the **Pacific Ocean**, where lots of **tectonic plates** meet. More than **90%** of all the **world's earthquakes** happen here. You'll also find **half the world's volcanoes** here.

ASIA

NORTH AMERICA

AUSTRALIA

SOUTH AMERICA

Ring of fire

Big bangs

A 2009 **earthquake** in L'Aquila, **Italy** (pictured), killed **308 people**. The **biggest** earthquake ever recorded shook the **whole Earth** for days. The **9.5 magnitude** earthquake in Valdivia, Chile, on 22 May 1960, **killed** more than **1600 people** and caused a huge **ocean wave**, called a **tsunami**, that then killed **many more people** in **far-away** Hawaii, Japan and the Philippines.

They've got a crush on you

The **world's largest snake**, the green anaconda, can grow to **7.5m (25ft) long**. It is not quite as long as the **world's longest snake**, the reticulated python, but the green anaconda is **fatter** and up to **twice as heavy**, weighing up to a **whopping 227kg (550lb)**. Both snakes get their food by **wrapping themselves** around an animal and **crushing it to death**. They then **swallow it whole**, head first, so the legs go down smoothly. They can easily **open out their jaws** to gobble up animals **much wider** than themselves – even a **deer with big antlers** … and **even YOU!**

I FIND SNAKE CHARMERS HARD TO SWALLOW...

How charming

In the **Indian subcontinent** and **northern Africa**, snake charmers **play music to snakes** to try to **hypnotise them**. Not something you should **try at home**!

Fleet without feet

You **can't outrun** a **black mamba**, thought to be the **world's quickest snake**. It can slither at up to **20km/h (12mph)**. It is also Africa's **longest venomous snake**.

A real killer

It is thought that each year about **14,000 people** in Southern Asia, **11,000 people** in India and **many people** in Africa **die** after **being bitten** by **venomous snakes** such as **cobras** and **vipers**. This is not because these snakes are actually the **most venomous**, but because the **people can't get medical help** quickly enough.

10 most venomous snakes

And they are all from Australia, the **Deadly Snake Capital** of the Universe!
However, only about **three or four people a year die** in Australia from snake bites.
1 Inland taipan (it has enough venom to kill about 100 people) **2 Eastern brown snake**
3 Coastal taipan 4 Tiger snake 5 Black tiger snake 6 Beaked sea snake
7 Black tiger snake (a sub-species) **8 Death adder 9 Gwardar 10 Spotted brown snake**

SLITHERIEST

Sssnooping into the sssecret world of sssnakesss

It never rains in Arizona

At least it **rarely rains** in **Yuma, Arizona**, in the **US**. This small city is in the **middle of a desert** and is the **sunniest place in the world**. Out of **4456 hours of daylight** every year, the **Sun shines** for **4174 hours** – or about **94%** of the time!

Rain, rain, go away

Lloro in **Colombia** is the **wettest place on Earth**. It gets an amazing **13,300mm** (524in) of rain **every year**! It's not the wettest place on record, though. Back in **1860–61**, **Cherrapunji** in India received **nearly double** that amount: **26,470mm** (1042in).

Waves of destruction

The **2004 Boxing Day tsunami** was the **deadliest** and **most destructive** tsunami ever recorded. A **massive earthquake**, with the same power as **23,000 atomic bombs**, shook the **Indian Ocean**, creating a **huge tidal wave** that **slammed into** 12 countries, including **Indonesia**, **Sri Lanka**, **India**, **Thailand** and **the Maldives**. The tsunami **killed** more than **226,000 people** and left **millions homeless**. Tsunamis are most common in the **Pacific Ocean**, in countries on the **'Pacific Ring of Fire'**, which have lots of **volcanoes** and **earthquakes**. 'Tsunami' is a **Japanese word** meaning 'harbour wave'.

Fishiest thunderstorms

Almost every year, in **May** or **June**, a storm **rolls through** the town of **Yoro**, in Honduras. There is **lightning**, **thunder** and **heavy rain** for **two hours**. Once it is over, **hundreds of living fish** are found **flopping around** on the ground. **No one knows** for certain how they get there. The town holds the **Festival of the Rain of Fishes** (Festival de la Lluvia de Peces) to celebrate.

AT LEAST IT'S NOT RAINING CATS AND DOGS!

EXTREME WEATHER

Nature's fury unleashed

Light fantastic

They say **lightning doesn't strike twice** – but in **Venezuela**, lightning strikes **thousands of times** a night! For **10 hours a night**, about **150 nights a year**, the **angry** skies **hurl** up to 280 lightning **bolts an hour** over big, mysterious **Lake Maracaibo**. This **amazing 'catatumbo lightning'** can be seen up to **400km** (250mi) away.

Flash figures

No wonder they **hurt so much**! The **temperature** of a **lightning bolt** can reach **30,000°C** (55,000°F) – **five times hotter** than the **Sun's surface**. Lightning strikes the ground about **8 million times a day** – about **100 times every second**! Lots more lightning **flashes up in the clouds**, without even **hitting the ground**.

7 times lucky

American national park ranger **Roy Sullivan** was **hit by lightning seven times** between **1942** and **1977** – and **survived them all**.

White wash
Greenland isn't actually **green**. Much of it is **thick white ice!**

CAN'T WAIT TO TRY THOSE NICE GREEN SAUSAGES

Whoa, boa
Perhaps the **greenest snake** is the **emerald tree boa**. This slithery serpent **lives** in the **rainforests of South America** and can **hide very well** in the **lush green trees**, where it **waits for small animals** to come along. Then it **squeezes them to death** before **swallowing** them.

GREENEST
The great green globe in all its glory

Happy place
One of the **'greenest' countries** in **the world** is **Bhutan**, high up in the **Himalayas**. About **70% of Bhutan** is **covered in thick green forest**, and the country is also very good at **protecting its environment**. It **banned plastic bags and cigarettes** because they **make people unhappy**. The country measures its success by its **'Gross National Happiness'!**

Have a heart, or three

Cuttlefish have the **greenest blood** of **any animal**. They also have **three hearts** to **pump that blood** around their body!

Turning green

If you find yourself **eating green sausages**, you might be at a **St Patrick's Day festival**. That's when **millions of Irish people** all around the world eat **green food**, drink **green drinks** and wear **green clothes** to **celebrate** St Patrick arriving in **Ireland**. Held on **17 March**, St Patrick's Day is celebrated in **more countries** than **any other national day**.

Gem of a stone

The **most popular green gemstone** is the **emerald**. The **largest emerald ever found** is as **big as a watermelon** – called the **Teodora**, from **Brazil**! It is valued at over **US$1 million**.

SOMETIMES THE WORLD SEEMS TO PASS ME BY...

Mossiest mammal

Sloths live in the **jungles** of **South America** and **move very s-l-o-w-l-y**. They move **so slowly** that **algae grows on them**, turning their **fur green**.

King whiskers

You can see one of the **world's longest beards ever** in the **US Smithsonian Institution** – or at least **5.3m (17ft 6in)** of it. The **beard** belonged to a Norwegian man, **Hans Langseth**, who died in **1927**. Another **30cm (1ft) of his beard** was left on his face when it was cut off. Hans used to **roll his beard up** and **tuck it into his coat or vest**. It was about **as long** as the world's **longest snake**, the **reticulated python** of Southeast Asia – but at least it **never strangled anyone!**

Ring my neck

Kayan women in **Thailand and Myanmar** look like they have the **longest necks in the world**. This is because they like to wear **brass coils** around **their necks**. The rings **don't actually** make their **necks longer**, but instead **push down their collar bones**. Some girls **start wearing neck rings** when they are as young as **five years old**.

LOOKING THIS GOOD CAN BE A PAIN IN THE NECK

Longest and skinniest

The **world's longest animal** is the **bootlace worm**. It can grow to **55m (180ft)**. That's **twice as long** as the **world's largest animal** – the **blue whale** – and just a **bit longer** than an **Olympic swimming pool**. But the worm is **so skinny** you could **fold it up** and **put it in a box** only **18cm (7in) square**. It lives along the north-east **Atlantic coastline**.

Hold your tongue

For its size, the **tube-lipped nectar bat**, found in **cloud forests** in **South America**, has the **longest licker**: its **tongue** is **one and a half times longer** than the bat is. **If this bat was a cat**, it could **drink milk** out of a bowl **1m (3ft) away!** It uses its tongue to **lick up nectar from flowers**. When it isn't **using its tongue**, it keeps it **tucked away in its ribcage**.

LONGEST

The long and short of it all

The whole tooth

The **male narwhal** is nicknamed the **'unicorn of the sea'**. It is a type of whale, with the **longest, pointiest tooth**, which looks like a **tusk**. Its tooth grows up to **3m (10ft) long** – nearly as long as a **small car**. No one knows what it is for, but it is **rarely used for fighting**.

Only half asleep

When **flamingos** go to sleep, they do so one side at a time. When they want to have a **snooze**, they **lift one leg up** and **let that side go to sleep**. When they want to rest the other side, they swap legs. Simple! Some flamingos eat certain **algae** that contain a chemical that turns them the **brightest pink.**

Sharp shooters

An **eagle** soaring high in the air can spot a **rabbit** on the ground **1.6km (1mi) away**. It has **especially large eyes** and **special retinas** that let it see very sharply straight ahead, and also to the side. It can then **swoop down** on its unsuspecting prey at up to 200km/h (124mph).

BIRD BRAINS

Flighty facts from the featheriest kingdom

Extreme endurance

The **emperor penguin** is the **world's biggest** penguin. It lives in just about the **harshest environment on Earth**. These **plucky** birds waddle up to **120km (75mi)** across **snow** and **ice** to get to their breeding grounds. After **mum** has laid her egg, **dad** puts it on his **feet**, rests his **fat, feathery belly** on top to keep it warm, then **stands shivering** with **thousands of other dads** in the **freezing wind** and **snow** for **two months** while mum takes to the **ocean** to feed. **Mum** finally comes back and **vomits** up **food** for the chick that has hatched under dad's tummy. They then **take turns** raising the young chick.

Eggs-agerated egg-stremes

Growing up to **2.7m (9ft) tall**, the African **ostrich** is the **world's largest bird**. It also lays the **world's largest eggs**, which can weigh a whopping **1.4kg (3lb)** each – about the same volume as **24 chicken eggs**! The **world's smallest bird** is the tiny **bee hummingbird**, from **Cuba**. People often mistake it for an insect! You could put **4700** of its pea-sized eggs inside one ostrich egg.

Cash for quetzals

Quetzals are beautiful, colourful birds that live in **South America**. They grow such lengthy tails, up to **1m (3ft)** long, that they can't take off out of trees properly, because **their tail** sometimes **gets caught on branches**. The people of **Guatemala** love their quetzals so much they named their **money** after them.

Showiest bird

Male **peacocks** use their **beautiful** feathers to **dazzle** the ladies. Their tails are **so large** they can't fly very well, but they sure do **look handsome**!

SHUFFLE UP, Y'ALL

Let's skip dinner...
Fresh fish is **healthy** and **delicious**.
But **kept too long**, it **turns really nasty**.

Surströmming, from **Sweden**, is tinned **fermented Baltic herring**. The fermenting herrings can sometimes make the **tins buckle**. The tins are **banned on airlines** because they **might blow up**! Most people eat it outside because of its **hideous pong**.

Hákarl, from **Iceland**, is the **fermented flesh** of a **shark** that has been **buried in the ground** for three months, and **then dried** for six months **before it is eaten**.

Narezushi is a **Japanese delicacy** made from **salted fish** that is **fermented with rice** for four years.

QUICK, I CAN'T HOLD MY BREATH MUCH LONGER...

Curb your curd
In **France**, **smelly cheese** is **banned** on **public transport**. Époisses de **Bourgogne**, said to be the **world's stinkiest cheese**, is a **no-no** on buses and trains in Paris.

Heaven and hell
Durian is a **tropical fruit** that is said to 'taste like heaven and smell like hell'. Some people say it **smells like sewage or vomit**. The odour is **so foul**, durian is **banned on public transport** in most of **Southeast Asia**, where it grows. It does, however, **taste delicious**!

Monster's flesh breath

Most people try to **do something** about their **bad breath**, but **some animals** want it **as awful as possible**! **Komodo dragons**, from **Indonesia**, have **toxic bacteria** in their mouth, which **smells foul**. They also leave **rotting flesh in their teeth**, which **smells even fouler**. All that badness in their mouths helps **kill their prey** when they chomp into it.

STOP – OR I'LL BREATHE ALL OVER YOU!

SMELLIEST

Some of the stinkiest things on Earth!

Dead giveaway

Do you **like the smell of rotting flesh?** Some **insects do**, and that's why they love a **giant flower** called the **Titan arum**, or **corpse flower**. It smells like an **old dead body**. The insects visit the flower and **help pollinate** the plant. The corpse flower is the **biggest flower in the world** – up to **3m** (10ft) **high**. It doesn't bloom very often – maybe only **once every few years** – and when it does flower, the **stinky thing** only lasts for about **three days**. It grows on the **Indonesian island** of **Sumatra**.

I MIGHT BE UGLY BUT I'M FULL OF SOUL...

Spirits in the sky

When **Buddhist people** in the high mountains of **Tibet die,** they often get a **'sky burial'**. The ground up there is **too thin** and **rocky to dig graves**, so their relatives take the dead body to a special spot so **vultures** can come and **eat them** and **release their souls**. Quite often they **chop the dead person's body up** to make it **easier** for the **vultures** to **gobble them down**.

HIGH AND MIGHTY

Some highly interesting human and natural wonders

High there – welcome to my floating islands

High up in the **Andes Mountains**, on the border of **Peru** and **Bolivia, Lake Titicaca** was **sacred** to the **Inca people**. The lake is **one of the highest** in the world – 3811m **(12,500ft)** above sea level – and is **famous** for its **'floating' Uros islands**. Local people build the islands out of **grassy reeds** that **grow in the lake**. They **started doing this** so they could **move their islands** away from **danger** if they were **attacked**.

Cascade of angels

If you thought **Niagara Falls** was big – well, **Angel Falls** in **Venezuela** is **19 times as high!** The **world's highest waterfall**, Angel Falls is **even taller** than the **world's tallest building**. It was named after an **American pilot** called **Jimmy Angel**, who saw it in **1937** while **looking for gold**. It is **so high up** – nearly **1km (3200ft)** high – that it is often **shrouded in cloud**.

5 tallest buildings

1 Burj Khalifa, United Arab Emirates: 828m (2717ft)
2 Abraj Al-Bait Towers, Saudi Arabia: 601m (1971ft)
3 Taipei 101, Taiwan: 509m (1670ft)
4 Shanghai World Financial Centre, China: 492m (1614ft)
5 International Commerce Centre, Hong Kong: 484m (1588ft)

800m (2625ft)
700m (2297ft)
600m (1969ft)
500m (1640ft)
400m (1312ft)
300m (984ft)
200m (656ft)
100m (328ft)

1 2 3 4 5

Lethal to a point

The **golden poison arrow frog** is only **5cm (2in) long**, but it contains enough **venom** to **kill 10 adults**. That's why this **most deadly frog** is used by **South American tribes** to make their **poison hunting darts**.

I GET A BIG BUZZ OUT OF DRINKING YOUR BLOOD!

Annoying little killers

They don't have **big teeth** or **sharp claws**, but **tiny mosquitoes** are the **deadliest insect** or **animal in the world**. That's because they **drink our blood**, and at the **same time** they can pass on **deadly diseases** such as **malaria** and **yellow fever**. They may have **killed** as many as **46 billion people** – that's **half the number** of people **who have ever lived!**

Death Road

The **North Yungas Road** in **Bolivia** is known as the **Road of Death**, or **El Camino de la Muerte**, because about **300 people die** on it **every year**. It is probably the **most dangerous road** in the **world**. It is only **3.2m (10ft) wide** – and there are **no safety rails** between the road and a **600m (1830ft) drop** to the **valley below**.

Which bean slays witch

People accused of being **witches in Nigeria** had to **eat poisonous calabar beans** in an **'ordeal by bean'**. Most then **died a horrible death**. The ordeal is **now banned** – but the **beans still grow** … so whatever you do, **don't eat them!**

DEFINITELY DEADLY

Seriously, these things can ruin your life

Shoot a hole in one

The **world's deadliest golf course** is thought to be on the **border** of **North and South Korea**, at a **United Nations military post** called **Camp Bonifas**. The golf course **green** has **minefields** on **three sides**. A golf ball one person hit **exploded a land mine – kabooom!**

DON'T GET ME CRANKY OR I'LL KICK YOU TO BITS

This big bird is a real ripper

Cassowaries can't fly, but these **big birds** can give you a **deadly kick**. Their feet have **three toes – the middle one** is **long, knife-like** and able to **rip you open**. A **fast runner**, this **scary-looking bird** can jump almost **2m (6.6ft)** straight into the **air**. Luckily it is **quite shy**. It lives in **Papua New Guinea** and **northern Australia**.

Weight, there's so much more...

African elephants are the **heaviest land animals**. They can weigh up to **12 tonnes (13 tons)** – about as much as **a bus**. But elephants are **like ants** when compared to **blue whales**, the **heaviest animals ever**. These whales can weigh up to **190 tonnes (210 tons)** – that's as much as **three houses!**

HEAVIEST

A lighter look at some truly hefty things

HIS BUM LOOKS BIG IN THAT...

Nimble giants

Japanese sumo wrestlers are the **world's heaviest sportsmen!** They follow a **special diet** and **exercise plan** to make them **huge** and **strong**. During a match, the idea is to **push the other wrestler** out of the ring, or **make them touch the floor** with **their body** (only the **soles of the feet** are allowed to **touch the ground**). Often the matches **only last a few seconds**. In Japan, **sumo wrestlers** are **big heroes**.

Whole world of heaviness

The **heaviest thing in the world** is **the world!** It weighs about

5,940,000,000,000,000,000,000

tonnes (6,550,000,000,000,000,000,000 tons).

Bulky boatload

The **Seawise Giant** is the **heaviest ship ever**. Fully loaded, it weighed some **657,019 tonnes** (724,239 tons) – about the same as **550,000 small cars**. It was **so huge** it couldn't even sail in the **English Channel!** At **458m (1503ft)**, it was **longer** than the **Petronas Towers** in Kuala Lumpur, Malaysia, **are high**. It was scrapped in **2010** – for **heavy metal**, of course.

With a heavy head

The **heaviest heads around** are to be found on **Easter Island**, in the **Pacific Ocean**. These **giant stone heads** weigh up to **78 tonnes** (86 tons). Many of them were **carved on one side of the island** and **rolled to the other side** on tree logs.

DOES MY BUM LOOK BIG IN THIS?

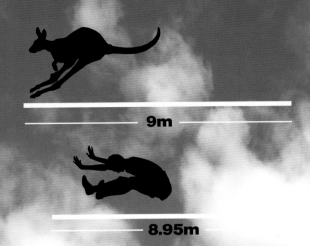

2.45m

5.4m

9m

8.95m

Animal vs human high jump record

The **human high jump** world record is **2.45m (8ft 0.46in)**.

WINNER: The mighty **American cougar** can leap **5.4m (18ft) high** – which means it could just about **jump up onto a giraffe's head!**

Animal vs human long jump record

The **human running long jump** world record is **8.95m (29ft 4.4in)**.

WINNER: A **male red kangaroo** can cover **9m (30ft)** with **each leap** – that's like jumping over a **killer whale**. It can also **jump 1.8m (6ft) high** – like leaping over a **tall man!**

HOP TO IT

It's great fun to jump and leap around

How many goats can you fit in one tree?

Lots! In the north African country of **Morocco**, goats are **nuts** about the fruit of the **argan tree**. They can't reach the **fruit** from the ground, so they **hop up into the tree** and **munch away**.

Tiny superpower

If we could **leap as high as fleas**, we could **jump right over** the **Washington Memorial** in the US **(169m/555ft)**. Fleas can jump **100 times their height!**

See-through trick

The world's most **see-through leaping animal** is the **glass frog**, which lives in the **South American rainforests**. You can see its **heart, intestines** and **liver** through its **clear skin!**

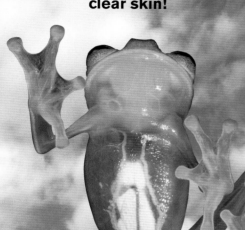

BABY BOOMS MAKE MY JOB MUCH HARDER!

Baby steps

Every year in June, in the **Spanish village** of **Castillo de Murcia**, dozens of **grown men dressed as devils leap over lines of babies** lying on blankets. **El Colacho**, or **baby jumping festival**, has been held every year **since 1620**. The **devils** are supposed to **take any evil vibes** from **the babies** as they **jump over them**, leaving the babies **pure**.

Great leap up

Maasai warriors from **Kenya** probably perform the **highest leaping dance** in the world. The dance is called the **adumu** and is **performed** when they **become adults**. The warriors **form a circle** and **take turns** to go in the middle and **leap as high as they can** to show **how strong they are**.

It's really good grub

You can find **plump white witchetty grubs** in the **trunks** and **roots** of **trees** in central **Australia**. Local **Aborigines snack on them**, either **raw** or **cooked**, and some **restaurants** even **serve them** as **delicacies**. When **cooked**, they taste a little bit like **chicken with peanut sauce!**

I'M TOO CHICKEN TO SHOW MYSELF ROUND HERE...

Hopping out for dinner

If people in **Dominica**, in the **Caribbean**, couldn't find mountain chickens, they used to enjoy eating the next best thing – 'mountain chicken frogs'. One of the **biggest frogs in the world**, they can weigh up to **1kg (2.2lb)**. But all that fine dining means **the frogs** are **now becoming rare**.

Dinner with a bite

Some restaurants in **Vietnam** serve up **cobra**. You can try the **still-beating heart** as a starter, before enjoying **cobra soup**, **cobra spring rolls** and **barbecued cobra**.

EGG with LEGS

Balut is known as the '**treat with feet**', and is a very **popular** street food in **the Philippines**. It is a **duck or chicken egg** that has been **buried in the ground** for a **few weeks**, so that the **baby bird inside** starts to form. The egg is then **soft-boiled** – and the **feathery insides** eaten with a spoon!

Ant that strange?

In the **Santander** region of **Colombia**, **giant ants** are a **popular snack**. The **heads**, **legs** and **wings** are **chopped off**, then the ants are **salted and fried**. They taste **smoky**, and **crackle** when you **crunch on them**.

FREAKY FOODS

When you're hungry enough, you might eat just about anything!

> I WISH THEY'D PIG OUT ON SOMETHING ELSE!

Pet for the pot

Some people like **guinea pigs as pets** – other people **like them with potato!** Guinea pigs are a **popular food** in **Peru** and **Bolivia** because they are **tasty**, high in **protein**, and **don't need much room** to be raised in.

Greatest reef ever

Australia's **Great Barrier Reef**, off the coast of **Queensland**, is the **largest living structure on Earth**. If you were up in the **International Space Station**, you could easily see it. The reef is more than **2600km (1616mi) long**. That's greater than the distance between **London and Moscow!**

The Great Barrier Reef
• is made up of **2900 individual reefs** and **900 islands**
• covers **35 million hectares (86 million acres)**
  – about the **same size as Japan**

It is home to:

30 species of whales, dolphins and porpoises

1500 fish species

350 coral species

6 sea turtle species

Sea-loving 'jumbos'

The **Great Barrier Reef** has one of the world's **largest colonies of dugongs**. More **related to elephants** than **dolphins**, peaceful dugongs are also called '**sea cows**' or '**sea camels**'.

COW? CAMEL? ELEPHANT? WHAT AM I?

Old beauties

Despite their size, **coral reefs grow very, very slowly** – only about **3cm (1.2in) every year**. Some coral reefs are more than **50 million years old!**

Animal, mineral or vegetable?

Coral reefs are made up of **really tiny animals** called **polyps**. The **wild colours** that you see in coral reefs come from the **billions of algae** that live in the polyps. The algae also **holds all the tiny polyps together** so they eventually form **big reefs**.

Beauty from destruction

In the **Solomon Islands**, sunken **wrecks of boats and tanks** from **World War II** are slowly being **taken over** by **coral reefs**. You can **dive down** and see the **rusty machines** covered in corals, that are now **new homes** to **thousands of colourful fish**.

I'M A BIGGER BRAIN THAN EINSTEIN'S!

Big brain in the drain

It's the **world's biggest brain**, but it is **not very smart**. In **Kelleston Drain**, off the coast of **Tobago** in the **Caribbean**, a brain coral measuring **3m (10ft)** by **5m (16ft)** sits around **thinking about not much at all**. It's called **brain coral** because it is **shaped like a huge piece of grey matter**.

RAINFORESTS OF THE SEA

Coral reefs are home to more plant and animal species than anywhere else on Earth, except rainforests. They take up an area half the size of France, yet hold a quarter of all marine life.

WHAT'S IN A NAME?

Strangely enough, every name tells a story

Happy heavenly city

You might know it as **Bangkok**, the **capital city** of **Thailand** – but you need to take a **big breath** if you wanted to give the city its **real name**:

KRUNG THEP MAHANAKHON AMON RATTANAKOSIN MAHINTHARAYUTHAYA MAHADILOK PHOP NOPPHARAT RATCHATHANI BURIROM UDOMRATCHANIWET MAHASATHAN AMON PIMAN AWATAN SATHIT SAKKATHATTIYA WITSANUKAM PRASIT.

It is the **longest place name** in the world. It means: **'The city of angels**, the **great city**, the **residence of the Emerald Buddha**, the **impregnable city** (of Ayuthaya) of God Indra, the **grand capital of the world** endowed with **nine precious gems**, the **happy city, abounding** in an **enormous Royal Palace** that **resembles the heavenly abode** where reigns the **reincarnated god**, a **city given by Indra** and **built by Vishnukarn.'** Most Thai people just call the city **'Krung Thep'**.

Say again?

The **US state of Massachusetts** is home to

LAKE CHARGOGGAGOGGMANCHAUGGAGOGGCHAUBUNAGUNGAMAUGG.

In a local **Native American language**, its name means something like: **'Englishmen at Manchaug at the fishing place at the boundary.'**

Tongue twister

The **world's longest one-word locality name** belongs to a hill in **New Zealand**:

ATAWHAKATANGIHANGAKOAUAUOTAMATEAHAUMAITAWHITIUREHAEA-TURIPUKAKAPIKIMAUNGAHORONUKUPOKAIWHENUAKITANATAHU.

It means: **'The summit** where **Tamatea**, the **man with the big knees**, the **climber of mountains**, the **land-swallower** who **travelled about**, played his **nose flute** to his **loved one.'** Got that?

Lion princesses

If you are a **Sikh girl** in the **Punjab** region of **India** and **Pakistan**, your **middle name** or **last name** will be **'Kaur'**, which means **princess**. If you are a **boy**, one of your names will be **'Singh'**, which means **lion**.

The **shortest place names in the world** are **A** in **Norway** and **Y** in **France**.

That's the spirit

The **Inuit** people of **Greenland**, **Alaska** and **Canada** give young babies a **soul name** called an **'atiq'**. The atiq is the name of a **loved older relative** who **has died**. They believe that **person's spirit** then **lives on** through the baby.

BOING BOING
NT, Australia

MONKEY'S EYEBROW
Kentucky, US

MIDDELFART
Denmark

MONSTER
The Netherlands

LOWER PIDDLE ON THE MARSH
Gloucestershire, UK

NOWHERE ELSE
Tasmania and South Australia

SCRATCHY BOTTOM
Dorset, UK

ELEPHANT BUTTE
New Mexico, US

ACCIDENT
Maryland, US

SMELLEY
Alabama, US

NOTHING
Arizona, US

BURRUMBUTTOCK
NSW, Australia

MUCKLE FLUGGA
Shetland Isles, UK

Jumbo pile-up on polo field

Giant piles of poo on the field are a **big problem** when playing **elephant polo**. The ball often **gets stuck in them** and someone has to **dig it out**! Elephant polo was **first played** in India **100 years ago**, when the **British** started using the **huge brainy beasts** instead of horses. There are **three jumbos** on each team. Each elephant has **two passengers** – one to **steer it** and one to **hit the ball** into the goal. There are **three major international tournaments** held during the year in **Nepal**, **Sri Lanka** and **Thailand**.

GLAD WE'RE NOT IN THE DUCK AGES ANYMORE...

Bumping off opponents

There's lots of **bumping going on** during the annual **camel wrestling** championship in **Selcuk, Turkey**. Two male camels **fight it out** for the right to **spend a little time** with a nearby lady camel. Although the **wrestling match** is often **quite tame**, the camels sometimes **take off** into the crowd, **scattering spectators**.

Duck out for a game

Pato, the **national game** of **Argentina**, is a mix of **polo** and **basketball**. The players **ride horses** – and in the old days they **used a duck** instead of a ball! Riders were **often trampled** under the horses' hoofs or **killed in knife fights** when the games got **too exciting**.

Mush, mush!

The **longest dog sled race in the world** is held every March in **Alaska**. Dogs taking part in the Iditarod have to run **1688km** (1049mi), **pulling a sled** through **blizzards** and **freezing temperatures**. The race **usually takes** between **9 and 15 days.**

ANIMAL CAPERS

Creatures big and small are extremely sporty

Slow and steady

The **slowest sport in the world** is **snail racing.** The slimy garden creatures start in the middle of a **33cm** (13in) **circle** and **'race' towards** the edge. The **record time** to complete the race is **2 minutes 20 seconds**!

Riding Big Bird

Ostriches are the **biggest birds in the world** – but did you know some people like to **hop onto their backs** and **race them?**

Ostrich racing is **very common** in **Africa,** especially in **Oudtshoorn**, in **South Africa**, where professional jockeys **jump on board**, then **hang on** to the bird's **feathers** and **neck** for **dear life** as they **race around** an oval track.

HOW DO YOU STEER THIS THING?

TOP 6 religions

1 Christianity About 2.2 billion people are Christian
2 Islam About 1.6 billion people are Muslim
3 Hinduism About 1 billion people are Hindu
4 Buddhism About 400 million people are Buddhist
5 Sikhism About 25 million people are Sikh
6 Judaism About 18 million people are Jewish

HOLIEST

Sacred sites of the world's biggest faiths

Big holy fig

Buddhists consider the **Bodhi Tree sacred**. It grows in a **temple** in the Indian town of **Bodh Gaya**, and is also called the **'Tree of Awakening'**. It is believed to come from the **same fig tree** that the **Buddha gained 'enlightenment'** under. Today, **many Buddhist pilgrims** travel there to **meditate**.

From far they Rome

St Peter's Basilica in **Vatican City** draws **millions of Catholic pilgrims** every year to Rome. It is considered the **largest Christian church** in the world. It can hold over **60,000 people inside its walls**, and covers **2.3ha (5.7ac)**. Its main ceiling dome is also **one of the largest** in the world.

Hindu heaven

About **90% of Indians** are **Hindu**. The Hindu **holy city** is **Varanasi**, in northern India, on the mighty sacred **Ganges River**, which Hindus consider to be a goddess called **Mother Ganga**. Every year, **millions of Hindus gather** along the banks of the Ganges, to **pray and bathe** in its **holy waters**. They **drink its water** and **scatter the ashes of their dead** in it.

Holiest hotspot

The **holiest sites** for **Jews** are the **Temple Mount** and the **Western Wall**, in Jerusalem. Jewish people **pray** in temples called **synagogues**. Their **spiritual leaders** are called Rabbis. **Muslims**, **Jews** and **Christians** all make pilgrimages to **The Holy Land** – a region that includes **Jordan**, **Israel** and **Egypt**.

The call of Mecca

The **holiest place** for **Muslims** is the **city of Mecca** in **Saudi Arabia**. Every day, **five times a day**, they **face towards Mecca** and **pray**. All Muslims must make a **pilgrimage**, or **hajj**, to **The Grand Mosque** in Mecca at least once. Every year, about **3 million people** do the **hajj**. In Mecca they walk around the **holiest building**, called the **Kaaba**, seven times. Muslims **pray** in temples known as **mosques**. Their holy book is the **Koran**.

Sikh and ye shall find...

For **Sikh** people, the **holiest place** is the **Golden Temple** at **Amristar**, in **India**, which is built over water. Sikhs **worship** in temples called **gurdwaras**. Each gurdwara has a **community kitchen** that serves **free food** to anyone. There are **no chairs** in the temples – everyone **sits on the floor** to show they are **all equal**. The Sikh holy text is the **Adi Granth**.

OH NO – I DROPPED MY BUCKET!

Washing days

It takes a team of **36 people three months** to clean all **24,000 windows** of the **160-storey Burj Khalifa** building in **Dubai**. It is the **tallest building in the world**, at **828m (2717ft)**, and is almost **twice as tall** as the **Empire State Building**. It is **so hot in Dubai** that the window cleaners **can only work** on the building's **shady side**.

170m
160m
150m
140m
130m
120m
110m
100m
90m
80m
70m
60m
50m
40m
30m
20m
10m

Tall for its age

California's redwood forests are **famous** for their **big trees**, but one **800-year-old giant** stands head and shoulders **above all the others**. **Hyperion** is the **world's tallest tree**. At **116m (380ft)**, it is **21m (70ft) taller** than the **Statue of Liberty** in New York City.

A bit toey

The **world's tallest statue** is **so huge** that **its toenails** are **higher than a person**. The **Spring Temple Buddha**, in **Henan, China**, is **128m (420ft) tall**. It is covered in **1100 huge pieces of copper**.

Inspiring

Ulm Münster, in Germany, was **once the tallest building in the world**; now it has to make do with being the **world's tallest church – 162m (531ft)**. There are **768 steps to the top** of the spire, but the **view is worth it**. During **World War II** the town around it was **flattened by bombs**, but the church was saved.

Wheel deal

The **tallest wheel in the world** takes **32 minutes** to **make one turn**. And you could be on it! It is the **Singapore Flyer**, a **165m (541ft) observation wheel** that **spins slowly** next to the **Singapore River**.

> I'M IN HIGH SPIRITS WHEN I TWIRL ON TIP-TOES

Tilting at stilts

Young men of the **Dan tribe** from the **Western Ivory Coast** may be the **world's tallest dancers!** They secretly practise for **3–5 years** to learn how to **twirl around** on **3m (10ft)** high stilts like **ballet dancers**, wearing a **sacred spirit mask**. Stilt dancers are called **'long spirits'**, as they are able to **talk with spirits.**

Loftiest legends

North American Indian tribes along the Pacific coast used **huge wooden totem poles** to tell their **stories, myths** and **legends**. The totems are still carved today.

TALLEST

Telling tales about tall things

Blowing hard and fast

King Fahd's Fountain, the **tallest fountain in the world**, at **Jeddah**, in **Saudi Arabia**, shoots water from the **Red Sea 312m (1024ft) into the air** – almost as high as the top of the **Eiffel Tower in Paris**. The **speed** of the water can reach **375km/h (233mph), faster** than a **Formula 1 racing car.**

By golly, it's enormous!

The **biggest spider in the world** is the **goliath bird eater**, which **terrorises wildlife** in **South America's jungles**. An early European explorer saw one **eating a hummingbird**, hence its name. Its **leg span** can be up to **28cm (11in)** – nearly as **long as a ruler**. Never fear, **it can't see very well**. Just as well!

EIGHT TASTY LEGS – THAT REALLY IS FAST FOOD!

Munching on spiders

Imagine being so hungry you could **eat a big, black hairy spider**. There was a time when people in **Cambodia** were so hungry that they **caught tarantulas in the jungle**, then **fried them whole – fangs and all!** – until **nice and crunchy**, but still a bit **soft in the middle**. Now people **visit the town of Skuon** to try them.

Tough stuff

For its weight, **spider web silk** is **five times stronger than steel**. If **we** could work out how to **spin a thread as tough**, we would be able to make a **bullet-proof vest** that could **stop a bomb!**

Spider diver

The **diving bell spider** can **stay under water all day** by creating a **bubble of air** in a **silk sack**. The bubble can **draw oxygen** from the **surrounding water**, like **gills in a fish**, but the spider needs to **race up to the surface** of the water every day **to grab a large gulp of fresh air**. It catches **little fish** instead of **flies!**

Come to mumma!

The **most motherly spider** in the **world** must be the **wolf spider**. The female **carries her eggs** with her until the **spiderlings hatch**. Then they **all hop onto mum's back** and **ride around** for a **couple of weeks**.

ONE MEASLY FLY, AND ALL THESE MOUTHS TO FEED

WEB SITES

A yarn or two about nature's best spinners

Pleased to meet you

The **happy face spider**, from **Hawaii**, may look like the **friendliest spider in the world**, but it really developed its **special markings** as a **camouflage** to **stop birds eating it**.

Quite a bite

The **most venomous spider in the world** is the **Brazilian wandering spider**. It has **enough venom** to **kill 180 mice**.

AND THEY SAY THIS BRIDGE IS THE BETTER ONE?

Ha-a-ang on!

The **Hussaini Hanging Bridge** in Pakistan is one of the **scariest rope bridges** in the world. That's because the bridge is **very old**, **very rickety**, **very narrow**, has lots of **missing planks** and gets **shaken wildly** by strong winds. Lots of people use it – but who knows **how many** actually **make it** to the **other side** ...

Race you to the bottom!

The **Hahnenkamm Downhill Race** in **Austria** is the **scariest downhill ski course** on the planet. It takes less than **two hair-raising minutes** for the world's best skiers to **zoom down** the **extremely steep** and **difficult** 3.3km (2mi) course, at up to **140km/h** (87mph)!

Horrible history

Museums can be **pretty interesting**, but some can give you a **real fright** – like the **Torture Museum** in Amsterdam, The Netherlands. It has lots of **terrifying contraptions** that were used to **punish really wicked** (and sometimes really innocent!) people back in the really **bad old days**. Things like the **head-chopping guillotine**, the **'rack'**, which **stretched a person** from both ends until their **bones popped out**, **interrogation chairs** covered in **skin-piercing metal spikes**, and the **'skull-cracker'** – a vice that **squashed a person's head** until their **brains oozed out** and their **eyes popped out** of their sockets! There are also torture museums in **Germany**, **Italy**, **the Czech Republic** and **San Marino**.

HAIRY SCARY

Not for the faint-hearted!

Fast roller

Riding the **world's fastest rollercoaster** – the Formula Rossa – is like being **flung off** the end of an **aircraft carrier** in a jet plane. It takes you from **zero to 240km/h** (149mph) in **less than 5 seconds** – the **same acceleration** as a **fighter plane**. It's at **Ferrari World** in **Abu Dhabi**, in the United Arab Emirates. If that's not **hairy enough** for you, try the **Kingda Ka rollercoaster** in **New Jersey**, US. You won't be there for a **long time**, and it might not be a **good time**, but it will be a **scary time**! The Kingda Ka is the **world's tallest** rollercoaster. From the top, the track drops **127m** (418ft) **straight down** – that's **twice as high** as Italy's famous **Leaning Tower of Pisa!** The cars reach **206km/h** (128mph).

Freaky rally

The **Dakar Rally** is a **dangerous** long-distance, off-road endurance motor race. **Trucks, cars, quad bikes** and **motorbikes** tear through the **desert for days** on end. Since it started in 1979, at least **49 people have died** in the race. The race used to go from **Paris,** in France, down to **Dakar** in the West African country of Senegal. In 2009, the race moved to **South America** because **wars in Africa** made it **even scarier.**

Petra

Rosy city really rocks

You might have seen the ancient city of **Petra** in the film *Indiana Jones and the Last Crusade*. Petra is on the edge of the **Arabian Desert**, in Jordan. Much of it, including **800 elaborate graves**, was **carved into rose-coloured rock** cliffs about **2000 years ago**.

Great Wall of China

Cloud-shrouded mystery

Up in the **highest mountains** of **Peru** sit the **stone ruins** of **Machu Picchu**. It is known as the **'Lost City of the Incas'**, because **nobody** except the **Inca people knew about it** until 1911. The city was **built from stone** around **1450 AD**, but was **abandoned** only 100 years later – **no one knows why**. The buildings were **so well constructed** that you **can't slip a knife** between the joins in the stones. The city was built from **huge rocks** hauled up the **steep mountains** over **great distances**.

Machu Picchu

Greatest wall EVER

The **Great Wall of China** is the **longest thing** people have **ever built**. It goes for about **8850km (5500mi)** – although not all of it is connected. Some parts were built more than **2000 years ago**, but the **most famous** bits were built between **1368** and **1644**. Bits of it have been **built and rebuilt many times**. When it was being built, it was nicknamed **'the longest cemetery on Earth'**, because **so many people died** building it.

7 MODERN WONDERS

The 'New Seven Wonders of the World' are truly amazing

Christ the Redeemer

He's one big dude

An **awesome statue** called **Christ the Redeemer** stands on top of a mountain and **watches over** the people of **Rio de Janeiro** in **Brazil**. The statue is as tall as a **10-storey building** and its arms are as **wide as two buses**. There are **small spikes** on the statue's head to **stop birds landing** and **making a mess**.

Chichén Itzá

Colossal day out

A day at the **Colosseum** in **Rome** was **quite a spectacle** almost **2000 years** ago. Rome's residents would **turn up** at the stadium, like we do for a **sporting match** today. In the morning they could watch **wild animals**, such as **lions, leopards, tigers** and **bears**, being **hunted** among movable buildings and trees. Over lunch they could watch **prisoners being executed**, then in the afternoon they could enjoy **blood-thirsty gladiator fights**. The arena was **covered in sand**, often **dyed red** to **hide the blood**.

Mayan marvel

The stone city of **Chichén Itzá**, in **Mexico**, was a **big centre** of ancient **Mayan civilisation** up to around **1200 AD**. You can still see its **huge pyramids** and **temples, star observatory**, carvings of **sacred feathered serpents, jaguars** and **warriors**, a **deep well** that people were **thrown into** to **please the gods**, and even **sports fields** where **brutal games** were played. The **most famous** building is the **Temple of Kukulkan**, which has **365 stone steps** – one for each day of the year. During the **spring** and **autumn equinox**, when the sun **hits the stone steps**, it makes a **shadow** shaped like **a snake**.

Colosseum

Taj Mahal

Monument to love

Imagine **loving your wife** so much you built one of the **most beautiful buildings** in the world for her **after she died**. That's what **Indian emperor Shah Jahan** did when his wife died in **1631**. His memorial to his wife, the **Taj Mahal**, took **22 years** and **22,000 people to build**. According to **legend**, Shah Jahan then had **the hands** of the architect and craftsmen **chopped off** so they could **never create another building** like it.

Drac's shack

You've heard of **Dracula**, right? Well that **blood-sucking fiend** is nothing compared to the **real-life bad lad** he was based on – a fellow called **Vlad the Impaler**, also known as **Vlad Dracula**, who **killed thousands of people** back in the 15th century by **impaling them on stakes**. Vlad the Impaler used to hang around **Bran Castle** in **Transylvania, Romania**, which is nicknamed **Dracula's castle**. You can **still visit** the castle today.

SPOOKY CREEPY

Things that might send a shiver down your spine ...

Cave graves

Watch out if you visit any **caves** in **Mali, Africa** – they might be **full of human bones!** The **Dogon** people have been **burying their dead** in them for **centuries**.

That's the spirit

In villages in some parts of **Southeast Asia**, such as **Thailand** and **Borneo**, residents build **'spirit houses'**, so that the **spirits** from the village have **somewhere to live**. If the people don't **look after them**, the spirits might **get up to no good**!

Tunnels of death

Paris in **France** may be the **'city of love'**, but it is also the **city of death**. Underneath its streets, in **old mine tunnels**, sit the **spooky catacombs**, which **hold the bones** of about **6 million dead people**, many of them arranged in **eerie patterns**. You could say it's the **dead centre of town**!

Hanging coffins

When **people die** in Sagada, in **the Philippines**, their bodies are often **placed in coffins**, which are then **hung off the side of cliffs**. It is thought that hanging the coffins **high off the ground** brings the dead person **closer to heaven**.

I'M HANGING AROUND HOPING FOR HEAVEN!

Sounding out a scene

Some animals, such as bats, **use sounds to 'see'** where they are going. They **make a noise**, such as a **click**, and **listen** for it to **echo off** whatever is around it. Their brains then **create a scene** from the sounds, just like **our brains do** from what **our eyes see**. This is called **echolocation**. A few **blind people** have also worked out how to use echolocation to 'see' — some can even **ride bicycles** and **go bushwalking**!

SOUND

Hear are some great ears

Owls have **amazing hearing**. They can **hear a mouse walking** 23m (75ft) away! Dolphins **use their ears** to hear — but they also **use their jaw**. Sounds make their **jaw vibrate**, and these vibrations reach their **inner ear**. Scientists think elephants can **feel sound** through their **trunk and feet**, as well as through their **great big flappy ears**.

Keeping eyes on the prize

Imagine being able to **spot a rabbit** sitting in the grass from **1.6km** (1mi) away! **Eagles** and other **birds of prey** can do this as they **soar through the air**. They can then **swoop down** at up to **200km/h** (124mph), while keeping their **target in focus** all the way.

BAD BREATH IS A CURSE WHEN YOU SMELL THIS WELL

SMELL

SIGHT

Sensational sniffers

Bears have a **better sense of smell** than any other land animal. They use it to **find food**, **a partner** and to help them **stay away from danger**. When polar bears are **hunting**, they can **smell a seal** under **1m** (3ft) of **ice**, from more than **1km** (0.6mi) **away**.

Animal magnetism

Sea turtles could be the oceans' **greatest navigators**. They **hatch from eggs** their mum **buried in the sand** on beaches around the world. After they are born, they travel up to **4800km (3000mi) across the oceans** in search of food and friendship. But when they are ready to **lay their own eggs**, the sea turtles will **swim back** to the **same beach they were born on!** Scientists think the turtles have **magnetic crystals** in their brains and use the **Earth's magnetism** and an **inbuilt map** to navigate.

SIXTH?

MAKING SENSE

Super senses of the animal kingdom

Touchy tasty

A **catfish** doesn't even need to **eat something** to know whether it tastes good or not. The fish has **'whiskers'** around its mouth, which **'taste'** things they touch. The catfish also has **very sensitive skin** that can **'smell'** chemicals in the water!

I WONDER WHAT THOSE WORDS TASTE LIKE?

TASTE

Blind mole's star attraction

It may **look weird**, but the **star-nosed mole** uses the **22 little 'fingers'** on its nose to **feel its way** around its dark and wet home. It is **almost blind**, so it **'sees'** with its nose. The mole's **pink starry nose** also lets it **quickly decide** whether something it touches **is tasty**, even underwater. It can **find and eat food faster** than any other animal.

TOUCH

Top 5 mobile phone users
Worldwide over 5.6 billion

1 China
1,010,000,000

2 India
903,727,208

3 United States
327,577,529

4 Indonesia
250,100,000

5 Brazil
245,200,000

Top 5 telephone line users
Worldwide 1,268,000,000

1 China
269,910,000

2 USA
141,000,000

3 Germany
48,700,000

4 Japan
47,579,000

5 Russia
44,200,000

CHATTY PLANET

News sure travels fast, and far!

Top 10 friendliest Facebook countries

1 US 155,920,760
2 India 45,048,100
3 Indonesia 43,515,080
4 Brazil 42,206,120
5 Mexico 33,597,260
6 Turkey 31,526,840
7 UK 30,485,180
8 Philippines 27,724,040
9 France 24,104,320
10 Germany 23,251,200

Top 5 internet users

1 China	485 million	(23% of world)
2 US	245 million	(12% of world)
3 India	100 million	(4.7% of world)
4 Japan	99 million	(4.7% of world)
5 Brazil	76 million	(3.6% of world)

Answer yourself

If you live in the **United Arab Emirates**, you can **phone yourself** up. There are 'only' **11,540,000 mobile phones** in the country, but that's enough for **every person** who lives there to **have two phones**.

From: Lonely Planet
To: You
Subject: How many people use email every day?

People around the world send **2.8 million emails every second** – or about **90 trillion every year**. Trouble is, about **90%** of them are **spam**. The **first spam email** was sent in **1978** and advertised a **new computer program** to scientists.

Dear Reader,

Hi, how are you? We are just writing to let you know that this letter is one of 400 billion letters sent every year throughout the world.

If you placed all the letters end to end, they would reach to the Moon and back 100 times! Or you could build a 4m (13ft) tall wall right around the world.

More people work for post offices around the world than live in El Salvador – about 6.2 million.

The US Postal Service is the largest in the world. It delivers about 6400 letters and packages every second, or 168 billion every year.

Yours sincerely

Lonely Planet

Sore thumbs

JTLYK, peeps in **the Philippines** r the **gr8est txt msgers** in the wirld. Evry day Filipiinos send **700 million txts** – mor thN **8000 evry 2nd!**

Hooves of thunder

The **largest animal migration** on Earth occurs on the **Serengeti plains in Africa**, when more than **2 million wildebeest and zebras** leave **Tanzania** for the **lush green grass** of the Masai Mara region of neighbouring **Kenya** in March. About **250,000 animals will die** on the way – some of them chomped by **hungry crocodiles waiting** for them to **cross the Mara River**.

ON THE MOVE

A flurry of feet, fins, hoofs and feathers: globe-trotting critters

NOW WHERE DID I LEAVE MY BABIES?

Great red tide

Christmas Island, in the **Indian Ocean**, is home to **1400 people** and **50 million red crabs!** Mostly you don't see them, but **once a year** the crabs **leave their burrows** and **head for the sea** to lay their eggs – up to **100,000 at a time**. This **huge migration** covers the island in a **moving red carpet**. Then all the red crabs and their babies **move back inland again!**

I'M HUNGRY, MUM – ARE WE NEARLY THERE YET?

70 000 KM

It's a long way home

Could you find your way back to your **front door** if you had just spent **five years** travelling **halfway around the world? Pacific salmon can!** The salmon leave the rivers where they are born, to live in the Pacific Ocean for **four or five years**, before they **return to the same river** to lay eggs. Amazingly, they don't simply return to their **same river**, they also **return to the exact spot on the river** in which they were born.

3 000 KM

Tern for the better

Arctic terns are the **world's greatest commuters.** Every year, these **tiny birds** fly from **Greenland** and **Iceland**, up near the **North Pole**, to feed at the very **bottom of the world**, in the **Antarctic**. They fly about **70,000km** (43,500mi) every year – that's almost **twice around the world!**

6 000 000 KM

Gliding to the Moon

An **albatross** might fly more than **16,000km** (10,000mi) to **deliver one meal** to its chick. But it doesn't get too tired. Its **huge wingspan** – up to **3.5m** (11ft) – means it can **glide for hours without flapping**. By the time it is **50 years old**, an albatross will have **flown at least 6 million km** (3.7 million mi). The average distance between the **Earth and the Moon** is **384,403km** (238,857mi) … so this means an albatross could have **flown to the Moon and back eight times, hardly flapping its wings!**

6 000 KM

Caribou come through

Every year, **huge herds of reindeer**, called **caribou**, charge across the Arctic areas of **Canada** in search of **food** and to **avoid wolves**. Some groups travel **6000km** (3700mi) a year – **further than** any other **mammal on Earth.**

Froggy smoothie

Big wrinkly frogs from **Lake Titicaca** in **Peru** are **unique** and **under threat**. The **funny folds** in their **skin** absorb **oxygen** from the water, letting them **breathe underwater**. But that's not why they are in trouble. Locals think they are **good for their health**. They **use a blender** to turn them into **soup** and then **drink them!**

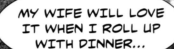

MY WIFE WILL LOVE IT WHEN I ROLL UP WITH DINNER...

Waste of a life

Imagine living your **WHOLE LIFE** up to **your knees in poo!** Dung beetles **couldn't be happier** than when they have lots of **fresh animal manure** to live in. They **eat some** of it, and they **bury the rest** of it. On a **good day**, a dung beetle can bury **250 times its own weight** in dung.

YUCKIEST

Don't look now – these things are really disgusting!

It's a mitey planet

You might **think you are clean**, but your body is **crawling with tiny creatures**, so **small** you can't even **see** them. There are more than **5000 creatures** living on **every 1 sq cm** (0.2 sq in) **of your body!** Your skin is **home to more critters** than there are **people on the planet**.

A rotten surprise

Next time you get **served something** you're **not keen on**, be **thankful** you're not **sitting down for dinner** in **Greenland**: you might be given **kiviak**. This is a **gutted seal** that is **stuffed** with **whole un-plucked seabirds** and then **buried under rocks**. After **a few months** the seal is **dug up**. The **insides** of the birds have **all rotted**. You **eat the guts** by **breaking off a bird's head**.

Slimy escape artist

Hagfish slip out of danger by producing a **hideous slimy gel** that **clogs their attacker's gills**, giving them time to **wriggle away**. Hagfish can **produce enough slime** to turn a **bucket of water to gel** in minutes. They can also tie themselves into a knot.

I'M HAVING THE SLIME OF MY LIFE!

I'M ONE TOUGH BEAR, I CAN LIVE ANYWHERE!

Bear with us...

Microscopic water bears can **live anywhere** and are probably the **hardiest animals** on the planet. They like to live in **moist moss** – but if the moss **dries out** they'll happily **go to sleep** until the moss **becomes wet again**. Some water bears **sleeping in dried moss** that had been **in a museum** for **100 years woke up** when the moss was moistened! They'll also **survive** being **boiled**, **frozen**, **shot into space**, **irradiated**, **poisoned** and **suffocated**.

ANIMAL ABODES

Some critters live in the most curious places

Dig right in

Human botflies like to make their home **right under your skin!** The flies **lay their eggs on you** and when the eggs hatch the **maggots burrow under your skin** and **feed on your flesh**. They are mainly found in **Central and South America**.

When home is a real bummer

Living inside **another animal's bottom** might seem like the **worst home in the world**, but **pearlfish**, which live along **Australia's Great Barrier Reef**, seem to find it **quite all right**. The pearlfish makes its home **inside a sea cucumber's bum** because it's a **good spot to hide** from predators.

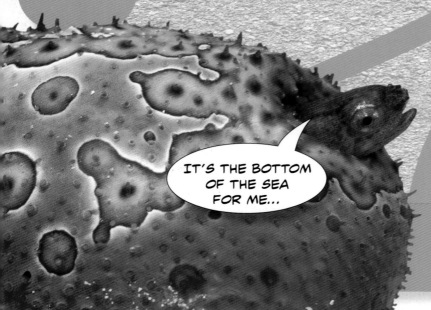

IT'S THE BOTTOM OF THE SEA FOR ME...

Branching out

You have to wonder if **killifish**, which live in the mangrove swamps of **Belize** and the **US state of Florida**, really **think they are birds**. The strange fish spend **a few months** every year **breathing air** and **living in trees**, when the **muddy pools** they normally swim in **dry up**.

The high life

High up in the **sky** live **tiny things**. Scientists have found **bacteria, fungi** and **viruses** living up to **18km** (11mi) above the **Earth**. That's **twice as high** as the **bar-headed goose** can fly (see page 168). But you **wouldn't want to be** flying around with them. Some of these **bugs can kill you!**

Ant antics

Ants might have the **busiest** and **biggest homes** in the world. One **massive colony** of ants on the **Mediterranean coast** is more than **6000km** (3728mi) **long** and contains **billions and billions** of ants.

Some like it hot

Giant tube worms like to bed down among **toxic chemicals, boiling temperatures** and **extreme pressure, 2500m** (8200ft) **below** the surface of the **ocean**. The worms live in **hard tubes** right next to **volcanic vents** on the ocean floor and **feast on bacteria**.

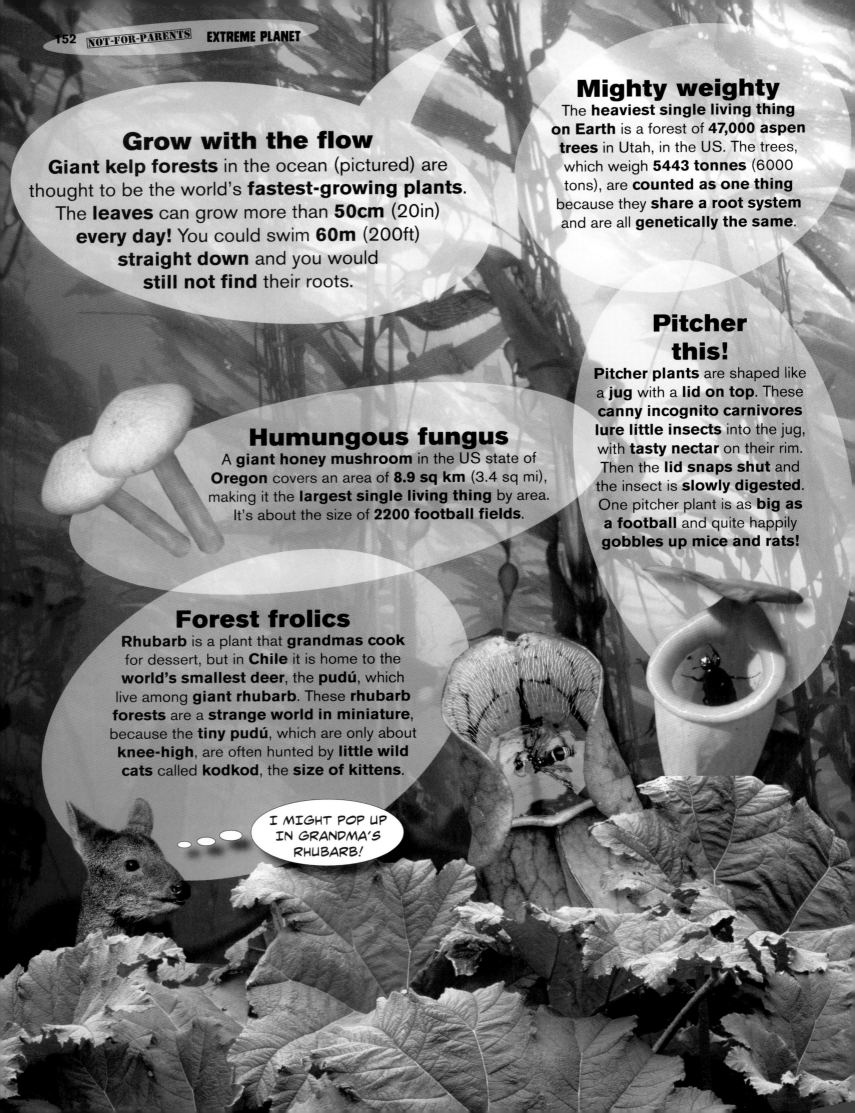

Grow with the flow
Giant kelp forests in the ocean (pictured) are thought to be the world's **fastest-growing plants**. The **leaves** can grow more than **50cm** (20in) **every day!** You could swim **60m** (200ft) **straight down** and you would **still not find** their roots.

Mighty weighty
The **heaviest single living thing on Earth** is a forest of **47,000 aspen trees** in Utah, in the US. The trees, which weigh **5443 tonnes** (6000 tons), are **counted as one thing** because they **share a root system** and are all **genetically the same**.

Pitcher this!
Pitcher plants are shaped like a **jug** with a **lid on top**. These **canny incognito carnivores lure little insects** into the jug, with **tasty nectar** on their rim. Then the **lid snaps shut** and the insect is **slowly digested**. One pitcher plant is as **big as a football** and quite happily **gobbles up mice and rats!**

Humungous fungus
A **giant honey mushroom** in the US state of **Oregon** covers an area of **8.9 sq km** (3.4 sq mi), making it the **largest single living thing** by area. It's about the size of **2200 football fields**.

Forest frolics
Rhubarb is a plant that **grandmas cook** for dessert, but in **Chile** it is home to the **world's smallest deer**, the **pudú**, which live among **giant rhubarb**. These **rhubarb forests** are a **strange world in miniature**, because the **tiny pudú**, which are only about **knee-high**, are often hunted by **little wild cats** called **kodkod**, the **size of kittens**.

I MIGHT POP UP IN GRANDMA'S RHUBARB!

PLANT PLANET

Wonders of the plant world

VIP killer

One **tasty-looking death cap mushroom** contains **enough poison** to **kill a grown-up.** Some people **accidentally eat it,** because it **looks like** other safe mushrooms. **Fatal mistake!** Scientists think it is responsible for **most mushroom poisonings** in the world. Native to **Europe** and **Asia**, the mushroom has killed **Popes, Roman emperors** and **royalty**.

Pretty large, in general

The **largest tree in the world** is **General Sherman**, a **giant sequoia** in the US state of **California**. It is not the **tallest** or the **widest**, but it has the **most volume of wood** in it. In northern California there are **coast redwoods so large** that **roads** have been **built through them!**

IT'D TAKE AN ARMY TO FELL THIS GENERAL...

Taste for waste

- About **1.18 billion tonnes** (1.3 billion tons) of food is **wasted** or **lost every year** – that's roughly **one-third** of **all the food** that is produced worldwide each year.
- That's about the same weight as **150 million elephants**, or **three times** the weight of **every person on the planet!**
- The world produces **enough food** to **feed twice as many people** who live on it – yet **1 billion people** are **under-nourished**.

Paddocks of pizza

Americans eat more than 7.3ha (18ac) of pizza every day!

FOOD FRENZY

Flashiest fast food facts

Cold cash

If you have a spare **US$25,000**, you might like to **treat yourself** to an **ice cream sundae** from the **Serendipity 3** restaurant in **New York**. It is the **most expensive dessert** in the world. It not only contains **nice ice cream** and **chocolate**, it is **infused with edible gold** and served in a **gold-plated goblet studded with diamonds**. Serendipity 3 also sells a **$69 hot dog**.

Percentage of people who eat fast food at least once a week

61% Hong Kong
59% Malaysia
54% Philippines
50% Singapore
44% Thailand
41% China
37% India
35% US
14% UK
3% Sweden

Big business
Every day, more than **600 million people** around the world spend **US$3 billion** on fast food. That's more than **$2 million every minute**. **McDonald's** serves over **50 million people a day** – more than the **entire population of Spain**.

Hungry colours
Yellow, red and orange are the **most popular colours** used in **fast food advertising**. That's because these three colours **make people feel hungrier**. And that means companies will **sell** more **burgers, pizza, chicken** or **sandwiches**!

Dung digs

Some **Maasai people** in **Kenya** build their **semi-permanent homes** from **cow dung**, which they **spread** over a frame of **sticks**. The houses look like **huge loaves** of bread.

Branch ranch

Have you ever built a **tree house?** The **Korowai** people of **Indonesia** live in the **biggest tree houses** in the world. Their **huge** homes **perch high** in the trees, **35m** (115ft) **above the ground**. You have to **climb up a rope** to get to them. The houses are well away from **swarming mosquitoes** and **nosy neighbours**.

Home really is a castle

Hundreds of years ago, rich or royal people in **Europe** and the **Middle East** built **huge** protective **forts** to live in, called **castles**. In the old fairytale stories, **princesses** lived in them and were **rescued by handsome princes**. The **largest castle** in the world is **Prague Castle**, in the Czech Republic. It's as **long as five football fields** and **twice as wide**.

Fairy-tale life

Some lucky people in **Cappadocia, Turkey**, get to live in **fairy chimneys**. The 'chimneys' are **soft rocks** that are part of **ancient volcanoes**. They have been shaped by erosion into **tall columns** with **little 'hats'** on top. Locals started **carving homes** and **churches** out of the rock about **2000 years ago**. Some of the fairy chimneys have been **turned into hotels**, so tourists can **stay in them** too.

Hiding from the heat

It gets **so hot** in the South Australian mining town of **Coober Pedy** that almost everyone **lives underground**. People have dug **homes**, **churches** and even **motels** into the dirt. **Golf** is a **popular sport**, but to **escape the heat,** they **play it at night**, above the ground, with **glowing balls!**

Comfy caves

Residents in the **Iranian village** of **Kandovan** have found a **natural way** of keeping **warm** in winter and **cool** in summer: **they live in caves!** Locals first started to **dig shelters** in the rocks hundreds of years ago to **escape the Mongol army**, then decided to stay. Most homes are **two or three storeys high** and have **rooms**, **verandas**, **windows** and **doorways** carved into the rocks.

HOME SWEET HOME

Some people live in the most way-out digs

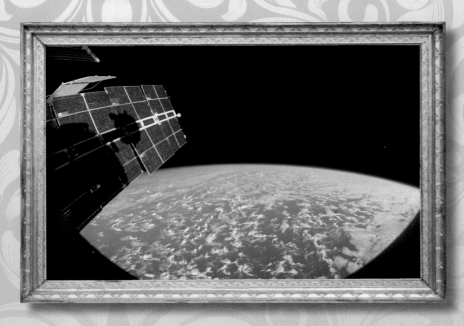

Best view ever

It's a room with a **space-age view,** and **no neighbours** in sight. The **International Space Station** is a spacecraft that **orbits the Earth**. People have **lived in it** since **2000**. The space station is as **big as a five-bedroom house** and has **two bathrooms**, a **gym** and **large windows**, so the **six people** who live in it can **look out** and **see Earth.** There is also a **laboratory** where the space crew **do experiments.**

DAD ALWAYS SAID I WAS 'OFF THE PLANET'!

Dark side of the Moon

When **Apollo 13** rounded the **far side of the Moon** on **15 April 1970**, its three astronauts, **James Lovell**, **John Swigert** and **Fred Haise**, were **401,056km** (249,205mi) **from Earth** – the **furthest away** anyone has **ever been**.

OUT OF THIS WORLD

Star attractions from the galaxy and beyond

Seeing little green men

Each year in July, **aliens** descend on the **town of Roswell** in the **US**. The scary **extra-terrestrials** are really only **people dressed up** as **space creatures** to attend the **Roswell UFO Festival**. Roswell was where some people say a **flying saucer crashed** one night in 1947.

A taste of space

How would you like to **float above the Earth**, just like **an astronaut?** That's what happens during **'zero gravity' flights**, where a **plane flies** in a **big semicircle** to **counteract gravity**. The **US** and **Russia** used zero gravity flights to **train their astronauts**, but now **anyone** can find out what it's like to travel in a **'vomit comet'** – if they have **enough money**, and a **strong stomach!**

I CAN'T GRASP THE GRAVITY OF MY SITUATION

Pocket rocket money

If you are **going into outer space** on a rocket, don't forget to take a **Quid** or two. **Scientists** have designed money, called the **Q**uasi **U**niversal **I**ntergalactic **D**enomination, or Quid, to be used by **space travellers**.

Lodger from outer space

The **Hoba** is a **giant 60 tonne** (67 ton) **iron meteorite** that landed in **Namibia**, Africa, about **80,000 years ago**. It is the **largest meteorite** ever found.

Eyes on the skies

The world's **largest optical telescope** scans the skies from the **Canary Islands**, in the **Atlantic Ocean**. The telescope has a mirror **10.4m** (34ft) **wide**. A **new European telescope** that is still being built will have a **lens as wide** as **five buses placed end to end**, and will contain **more glass** than **all the other telescopes** in the world **combined**. It will be **so powerful** that **astronomers** will be **able to see** the **lunar rover** that was **left on the Moon** in 1971.

Look, up in the sky!

What goes up doesn't **always** come down. In the sky there are **hundreds of thousands** of bits of **old space rockets** and **satellites circling the Earth**. The International Space Station almost got **walloped** by some bits in 2011, and the astronauts living there got ready to leave. But sometimes the **space junk** *does* **come down**. Lottie Williams, from **Oklahoma** in the US, was **struck on the shoulder** by a piece of an **old rocket** that fell from the sky in 1997. She was not harmed.

System crash

Ever wonder where our old computers and mobile phones get to? Chances are they'll end up in **Guiyu**, in **China**. More than **150,000 workers** pull old computers apart, to **recycle the metal and parts inside**, then **burn** what's left over. But many of these bits are **toxic**. So is the **smoke from the fires**, which has **poisoned the city** and the **people who live there**.

Lot of bottle

Tomislav Radovanovic, from **Serbia**, has found a great way to use up **old plastic drink bottles** – he's built a **house** from them. He's even used different **coloured** bottles to make patterns in the walls. Even the **kitchen furniture** is made from bottles! The only part of the house not made from plastic bottles is the floor.

730kg
per person
every year

UNITED STATES

920kg
per person
every year

HONG KONG

Garbage greatness

The **US** produces more rubbish than anywhere else in the world. About **230 million tonnes (254 million tons)** of garbage piles up every year – about **730kg (1600lb) for every citizen**. That's **40% of the world's waste**. However, people living in **Hong Kong** produce the most waste per person: **920kg (2000lb)**.

Dark side of the Moon

Earthlings have visited the Moon six times. This is some of what they have left behind: **6 lunar modules, 6 American flags, 3 electric lunar rovers, boots, camera gear, a hammer, a feather, a piece of the Wright brothers' plane, scientific instruments, a telescope, 3 laser reflectors and 3 golf balls.**

Watery grave

The **biggest** load of rubbish in the world is the **Great Pacific Garbage Patch**, a **100 million tonne (110 million ton)** mass of **junk** in the **Pacific Ocean** between **California** and **Japan**. It is mainly bits of **plastic**, and scientists think it could cover an area of ocean as big as the US. **Wind and currents** round up all the **garbage** in the surrounding ocean and dump it here.

WHAT RUBBISH!

How we trash the planet … and beyond!

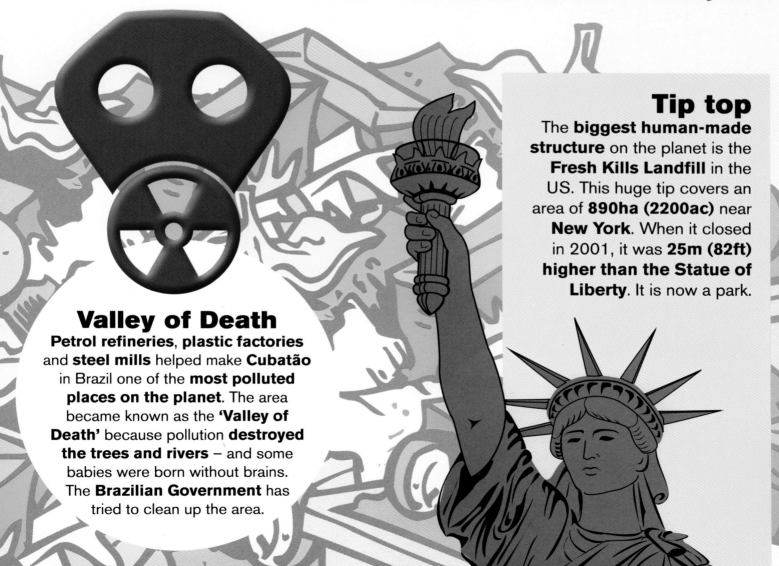

Valley of Death

Petrol refineries, plastic factories and **steel mills** helped make **Cubatão** in Brazil one of the **most polluted places on the planet**. The area became known as the **'Valley of Death'** because pollution **destroyed the trees and rivers** – and some babies were born without brains. The **Brazilian Government** has tried to clean up the area.

Tip top

The **biggest human-made structure** on the planet is the **Fresh Kills Landfill** in the US. This huge tip covers an area of **890ha (2200ac)** near **New York**. When it closed in 2001, it was **25m (82ft) higher than the Statue of Liberty**. It is now a park.

Two-legged lizard wizard

The little **Mexican mole lizard**, or **ajolote**, isn't really **a lizard** at all, although it is a **close lizard relative**. It looks more like a **worm** – except for its **two lizard-like legs**, right up **near its head**. It lives **underground** in **little tunnels**, using its **claws to shuffle** through soil and find **yummy grubs** and **insects** to eat.

Turbo powered

Unlike other fish, the **fist-sized psychedelic frogfish** doesn't have **scales**. Instead, it has **fleshy, flabby skin**. Also, unlike other fish, **it can't swim**. Instead, it **bounces around the sea floor**, on its **blobby foot-like fins**. It also uses **jet propulsion** to **spurt about** all over the place, by **shooting water** through its **gills**. This **aqua-eyed curiosity** was only **discovered** in 2008.

KOOKY CRITTERS

The most curious creatures around

I'M THE ONE COPPING ALL THE BAD LUCK ROUND HERE...

Aye yay yay!

The **aye-aye** is the **world's largest** – and probably **freakiest** – **nocturnal primate**. It **lives only** on the island of **Madagascar**, **high up in trees**. It taps its **long, skinny middle finger** on trees, looking for **tasty grubs**, which it **scoops out** with its long finger. Aye-ayes are **dying out** because local people **kill them**, thinking they **bring bad luck**.

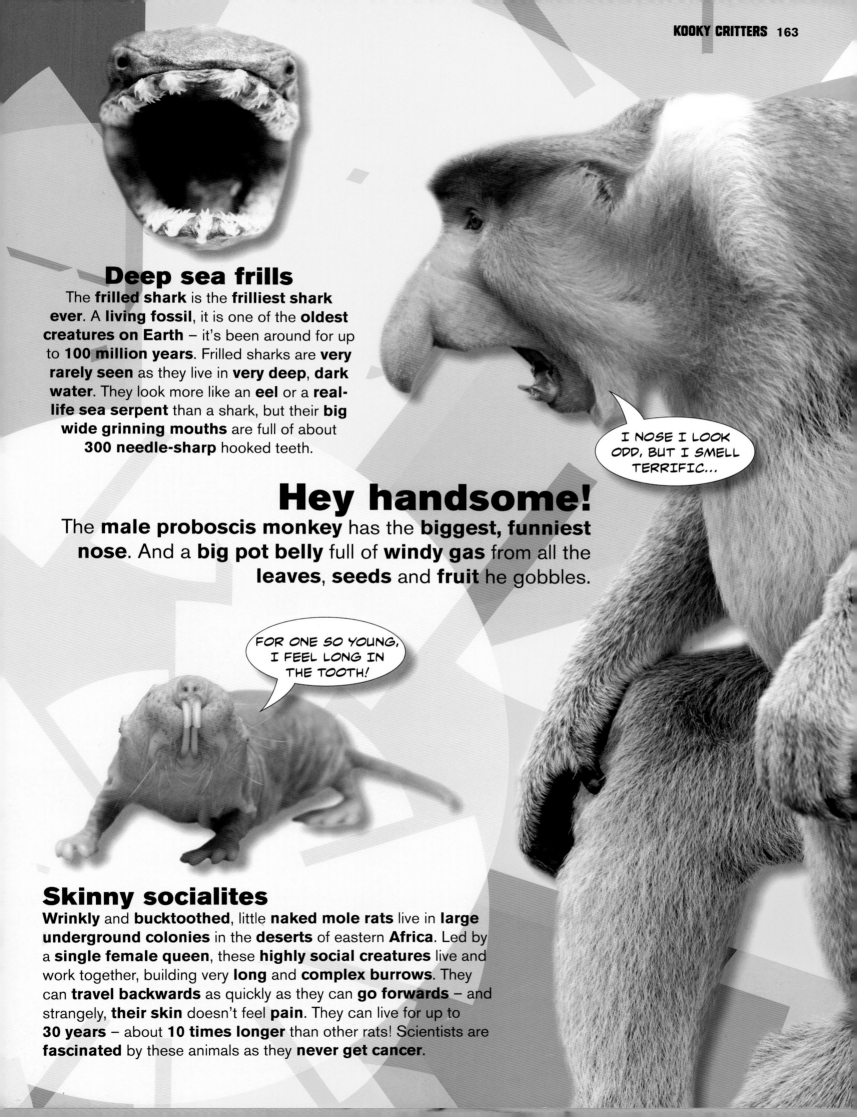

Deep sea frills

The **frilled shark** is the **frilliest shark ever**. A **living fossil**, it is one of the **oldest creatures on Earth** – it's been around for up to **100 million years**. Frilled sharks are **very rarely seen** as they live in **very deep**, **dark water**. They look more like an **eel** or a **real-life sea serpent** than a shark, but their **big wide grinning mouths** are full of about **300 needle-sharp** hooked teeth.

I NOSE I LOOK ODD, BUT I SMELL TERRIFIC...

Hey handsome!

The **male proboscis monkey** has the **biggest, funniest nose**. And a **big pot belly** full of **windy gas** from all the **leaves**, **seeds** and **fruit** he gobbles.

FOR ONE SO YOUNG, I FEEL LONG IN THE TOOTH!

Skinny socialites

Wrinkly and **bucktoothed**, little **naked mole rats** live in **large underground colonies** in the **deserts** of eastern **Africa**. Led by a **single female queen**, these **highly social creatures** live and work together, building very **long** and **complex burrows**. They can **travel backwards** as quickly as they can **go forwards** – and strangely, **their skin** doesn't feel **pain**. They can live for up to **30 years** – about **10 times longer** than other rats! Scientists are **fascinated** by these animals as they **never get cancer**.

Birth of Earth

The **oldest piece of earth on Earth** is the Jack Hills in Western Australia (pictured). They are more than **3.6 billion years old**. The rocks in the Jack Hills contain bits of a mineral called **zircon** that are **4.4 billion years old** – only **slightly younger** than the **Earth itself**.

OLDEST

Truly old things on and of the Earth

Clammy contenders

Some **clams** living in the **icy waters** off **Iceland** are more than **400 years old**. That means they were **sitting around** on the bottom of the ocean when **William Shakespeare** was writing his **famous plays**. Scientists work out the age of clams by **counting the rings** on their shells.

Can't match this patch

A **patch of seagrass** in the **Mediterranean Sea** could be the **oldest living thing on Earth**. Scientists reckon the seagrass could be more than **100,000 years old**. It **never dies** because it **keeps making clones** of itself!

IT'S NOT SO SHELLFISH TO LIVE THIS LONG!

The **oldest person** ever known was **French woman** Jeanne Calment. She died in 1997, aged **122 years, 164 days**.

You're only as old as you feel – I feel 180!

Slow and steady

Giant tortoises can live a very long time, **much longer** than humans. **Jonathan** is a **Seychelles giant tortoise** that lives on the island of **Saint Helena**, and is the **oldest living land animal**. He was born in **1832** – so he's **much older** than even your grandparents. **Planes** and **cars** and **movies** hadn't even **been invented** back then!

Golden oldies

Macaw parrots can live for over **80 years**.

New Zealand **Tuatara lizards** can live for over **100 years**.

Some **koi fish** can live for over **200 years**.

Bowhead whales can live up to **200 years**.

With your body and my brain we could go places

Cheating death?

Some people have themselves **frozen when they die**, hoping that **one day** there will be **a cure** for whatever **killed them**. This is called **cryonics**. It is **expensive**, so some people just have their **brain stored**. Dr James Bedford was the **first person** to have his **body preserved**, in 1967. If he is **ever revived**, maybe he could live to be the **oldest man** on Earth!

Raising the bar

No other birds **fly higher** than **bar-headed geese**, which sometimes wing their way over the world's tallest peak, **Mt Everest**, which is **8848m (29,029ft) high**. It takes them about **8 hours**.

FLYING THIS HIGH IS A BIT OVER THE TOP!

Lot of hot air

Every November, near **Saga City** in **Japan**, **hundreds of brightly coloured** and **oddly shaped balloons** take to the sky. The **Saga International Balloon Festival** is the **largest aerial event in Asia**, and one of the biggest balloon festivals in the world. **The biggest balloon festival** is held in **Albuquerque**, US, in October – more than **750 balloons** float above the ground during the **nine-day event**.

PEOPLE NO MATCH FOR SPEEDY GOOSE

While it takes a bar-headed goose about 8 hours to fly over the top of Mt Everest, it took humans **7 weeks** to scale the peak for the first time. New Zealander Edmund Hillary and Tenzing Norgay from Nepal became the **first two people** to reach the top of Mt Everest on 29 May 1953. They had to carry oxygen tanks because it's very **hard to breathe** up there.

Dizzy view

If you want to take **a lift into the sky**, try the **Bailong Elevator** in **Zhangjiajie, China**. It is the **world's highest exterior elevator**. It is **330m (1070ft) tall** and clings to the side of a cliff. Its glass-fronted cars give a giddy view straight down over a valley.

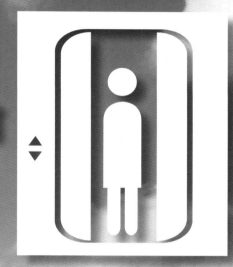

Clear clouds

You need really good eyes to see **the world's highest clouds**. They are **76–85km (47–53mi) above the Earth!** They are called **'night clouds'**, or **noctilucent clouds**, and are made of **ice crystals**. You can only see these beautiful clouds **just after sunset**, when the sun shines up on them from **below the horizon**.

UP IN THE AIR

It's a different world up there!

Flitting to fame

Pretty little **tortoiseshell butterflies** have been spotted fluttering about the **Himalayan** mountains, **5791m (19,000ft) above sea level** – making them the world's **highest-flying insects**.

Flying around the pole

'Pole flying' is an old ritual that the **Totonac** people in **Mexico** still practise. **Five men** in traditional costumes climb a **30m (90ft) pole**. One stays on top of the pole, **dancing on a tiny platform** and **playing a flute and drum**. The others, **strapped** to the pole by ropes, **jump backwards** off the platform, then slowly **'fly'** upside down around the pole, down to the ground. **Each of the four flying men represents a season**, and each flies around the pole **13 times**, signifying the **52 weeks of the year**.

PERFECTLY TINY

The world in miniature

Branching out

Imagine having a **whole forest** living in **your house**! Bonsai is a **Japanese art form** that grows **miniature versions** of **real trees**. Leaves are **pruned**, trunks are **trimmed** and branches are **wired** to make the **little plants** look just like the **real thing**. Some bonsai trees are only **3–8cm** (1–3in) high.

Itty bitty city

The **world's smallest nation, Vatican City,** covers an area about the size of **60 football fields** – only **44ha** (110ac). It has a **population** the size of a **secondary school** – **about 800 residents,** making it also the **nation** with the **smallest population** in the world.

Carving a name for himself

Willard Wigan, a **sculptor** from **England**, has a good eye. He needs to, as he makes the **world's smallest statues**. His creations include a **Statue of Liberty** that fits into the **eye of a needle**, and a copy of **Michelangelo's** famous **statue of David**, carved from a **grain of sand**. Pictured here is a **photo, taken through a microscope,** of his statue *The Starry Lovers*, perched **on top of a diamond ring**.

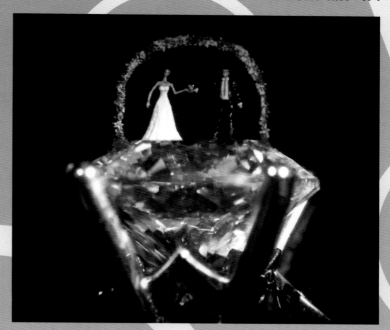

Thread bare

The **world's smallest snake**, the **Barbados threadsnake**, was discovered in **2008** on the island of **Barbados**. It **fits on a coin** and is **as thin as spaghetti**. It only grows about **10cm** (4in) long.

Buzz buzz bumble bird?

The **Cuban bee hummingbird** is the **world's smallest bird**. It is **so small** – only **5cm** (2in) long – that people often **mistake it for a bee!** It weighs a mere **1.8g** (0.06oz), and the **males are even smaller** than the females.

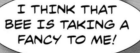

I THINK THAT BEE IS TAKING A FANCY TO ME!

A cupful of lemur

They could **easily fit in a teacup**, but **mouse lemurs** are our **not-too-distant cousins**. These **6cm** (2.5in) creatures, from the **island of Madagascar**, are the **smallest primates** in the world. They may soon **die out** because their **forest homes** are being **cut down**.

Slowly shrinking

Madagascar is also where you'll find the **world's smallest** chameleon. The **pygmy chameleon** is less than **2.5cm** (1in) long and could easily **sit on your fingertip**. It **started out** much bigger **thousands of years ago**, but **shrank** over time, probably because **food was scarce** on the island.

THAT LEMUR IS ONE BIG HAIRY MONSTER...

Grandest hole

The **Grand Canyon** (pictured) is one of the **biggest** and most **spectacular canyons** on Earth. It is certainly the **most famous!** It was carved by a single river, the **Colorado**, over **millions of years**. The main canyon is **365km** (227mi) long, **29km** (18mi) wide and up to **1.6km** (1mi) deep.

Place of pong

Hverir, in **Iceland**, is one of the **smelliest** and **strangest-looking** places in the world. It is where the centre of the Earth is trying to **force its way** to the surface. It is full of **steaming holes** in the ground, **weird rocks, sulphurous puddles** and **stinky mud pools**.

WILDEST LANDSCAPES

Some of nature's most extreme and fascinating creations

Another world

Visiting **Socotra Island**, in the **Indian Ocean**, might feel like **visiting another planet** – and in a way you are. The island has been **isolated** from the **rest of world** for **so long** that many of its **plants** have **evolved differently** to those found anywhere else. Check out these **dragon's blood trees!**

Knock on stone

The **Stone Forest**, or **Shilin**, in **China** is a **huge grouping** of **tall rock pillars** that **look like trees**. The stone forest covers an area as big as **25,000 rugby fields** or **baseball diamonds**. It was formed **270 million** years ago, before **dinosaurs** were around.

Ride 'em cowboy

Ever watched any old Western cowboy movies on TV? If so, **Monument Valley** in the US might **look familiar**, as it has appeared in dozens of **movies** and **TV shows**, and even in some **video games**.

Sweet, but don't eat

They look **good enough to eat**, but the **Chocolate Hills** in the **Philippines** would taste just like **limestone** if you **bit into one**. There are about **1700** of these almost **perfectly shaped** little hills. They are **covered in grass**, which turns **chocolate brown** during the dry season.

Growing into its legs

The **giant African millipede** is the world's **longest millipede**. It is **born with** only about **14 legs**. As it grows, it **adds more legs**. By the time it reaches its adult length – up to **38cm** (15in) – it can have as many as **100 legs**.

HMM, WHERE'S MY CLAM CHOWDER RECIPE?

One shell of a clam!

Most **clams** are **small enough** to **eat by the handful**, but **giant clams** are **big enough** to **swallow** a **small person whole**. Lucky for you, they **'clam up'** so slowly that you can easily **swim away** before this happens. That's probably why there are **no records** of anyone being **gobbled by a clam**. Not yet, anyway.

Super sea serpent

Nicknamed the **'world's biggest herring'**, the **oarfish** is the **longest bony fish**. It can grow up to **17m** (56ft) long. It takes about **15 men** to hold a **full-grown** fish up from **head to tail**. It isn't too **scary** though – **it has no teeth**.

Mum, I'm thirsty again

Human babies drink about **750ml** (25fl oz) **a day** – just a dribble compared to the **world's biggest baby**, the **blue whale**. Blue whale calves **gulp down 330 litres** (87.5 gallons) **of milk a day** and stack on about **90kg** (200lb) every **24 hours** – as much as a **large man** weighs! It's even **born huge** – almost as **long** as a **bus** and **heavier** than a **Rolls-Royce**.

Giants walk among us

Giant salamanders live in **Japan** and **China**. They are the **world's largest amphibians** – creatures that can live in water or on land. They can grow up to **1.8m** (5ft 10in) long – although one in the 17th century was supposedly **10m** (33ft) long and **ate cows** and **horses**! **Warts** on their bodies pick up **vibrations** that help them **hunt**.

An adult **elephant** can produce up to **80kg** (176lb) of **poo every day**.

THIS IS ONE OARSOME FISH!

WHAT A WHOPPER!

Giant stars of the animal kingdom

ANIMALS IN DANGER

Some creatures are in a whole world of trouble

Every day we lose about 135 plant, animal and insect species.

Name: Kakapo
Lives: New Zealand
Prefers: Native forests and woodland
Number remaining: about 125
Threatened by: Habitat loss; predation by dogs, cats and rats
Comments: World's heaviest parrot; can't fly; nocturnal. Active breeding programs underway

Name: Tiger
Lives: Asia and Indian subcontinent
Prefers: Mountains and forests
Number in wild: about 3500
Threatened by: Habitat loss; poaching
Comments: 3 tiger sub-species became extinct in the past 60 years. Hunted for use in Chinese medicine

Also threatened with extinction
Addax, Niger
Amur leopard, Russia
Blue-throated macaw, Bolivia
Iberian lynx, Spain
Saola, Vietnam and Laos

Name: Orange-bellied parrot
Lives: Tasmania and Victoria, Australia
Prefers: Coastal grasslands
Number in wild: about 20
Threatened by: Habitat loss; species competition
Comments: Active breeding programs underway

WANTED ALIVE

Name: Leatherback turtle
Lives: Pacific and Atlantic Oceans
Number remaining: about 2300 adult females in Pacific Ocean; Atlantic Ocean numbers are dropping
Threatened by: Marine pollution, especially plastic bags; fishing
Comments: Largest sea turtle; has survived 100 million years

ONLY A BIRD BRAIN WOULD LET ME VANISH!

WANTED ALIVE

WANTED ALIVE

WANTED ALIVE

Name: Javan rhino
Lives: Java
Prefers: Thick forests
Number in wild: about 50
Threatened by: Poaching; habitat loss
Comments: Last Javan rhino in Vietnam died in 2010. Its Asian relative, the Sumatran rhino, also highly endangered

Name: Bluefin tuna
Lives: Atlantic, Pacific, Indian and Southern oceans
Number in wild: 25,000 in Atlantic Ocean, and many tens of thousands in the Pacific Ocean – but fishing takes many thousands every year
Threatened by: Overfishing
Comments: A single tuna can sell for more than US$100,000. This is why 10,000 tonnes (11,000 tons) are still caught every year

Kissy kissy

In German-speaking countries, **Weiberfastnacht** is a **women's carnival night**, where ladies are allowed to **cut off a gentleman's tie**, and to **kiss any man** they like! It is part of a **bigger** German carnival called **Fasching**, **Karneval**, **Fastnacht**, **Fasnacht** or **Fastelabend**.

Calypso crazy

The **Trinidad and Tobago Carnival** in the **Caribbean** starts before dawn on the Monday morning before Ash Wednesday. People **smear themselves in mud**, **chocolate**, **paint** or **oil** and **run along the dark streets**, pretending to be **devils and imps**, and waking everyone up with **loud soca music**. Then follows **two days** of **calypso**, **steelpan** and **soca music contests**, and a **grand parade** where people wear **beautiful costumes** decorated with **feathers** and **sequins**.

Samba spectacular

The **Rio Carnival** is the world's **biggest party**, held every year in **Rio de Janeiro**, Brazil. The carnival lasts **four days**, with lots of **music** and **singing**, and finishes with a **huge street parade** called the **Samba Parade**, watched by **millions**. In the Samba Parade, **dance groups** try to **outshine** and **out-dance** each other, wearing the most **dazzling outfits** and creating the most **amazing floats**. Some groups have **hundreds of dancers** and up to **eight floats!**

Getting hitched in a big way

Hindu weddings can last **several days**. The **bride** is often dressed in **red** and **gold**, with beautiful **henna patterns** on her hands and feet. Quite often, **dozens of couples** get married **at the same time** in **one huge ceremony**. Flower petals are **thrown into the air** as each lucky couple is blessed.

PARTY TIME!

Some of the biggest celebrations on the planet

Monkey business

Those cheeky **macaque monkeys** in **Lopburi**, Thailand, **go ape** at the **Monkey Buffet Festival**. The monkeys are considered to be **holy**, so on the last Sunday in November, people give them a **big party**. They set up tables full of beautifully arranged **tropical fruits**, **vegetables**, **sweets** and **even drinks**, which the monkeys **gobble up**.

Somebody can't count

How long do you think **Nine Mile Canyon** in the US state of **Utah** might be? Well it's **not** nine miles, it is more like **40 miles (60km)** – and it is the **longest 'art gallery'** in the world. More than **10,000 figures** are **carved** into the **cliffs** of the canyon, most of them by **native Americans hundreds of years** ago.

ART ATTACK

A portrait of artistic extremes

Supreme brush with wealth

French artist **Paul Cezanne's** 1895 painting **The Card Players** sold for about **US$250 million** in 2011, making it the **most expensive painting ever**. Had the artist received all that money way back then, he would have earned about **$28,000 an hour** for painting it!

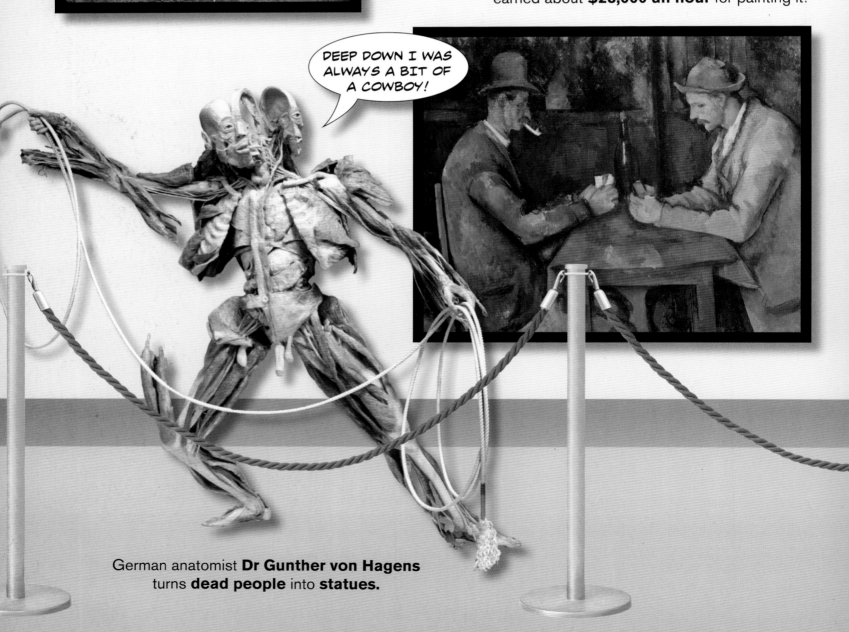

German anatomist **Dr Gunther von Hagens** turns **dead people** into **statues**.

Take time to look

The Louvre, in **Paris**, is the world's **most visited art museum**. More than **23,000 people** wander through it **every day**. It has **so many objects** on show that if you spent **2 minutes looking at each one**, it would take you **4 months** to **see everything** during opening hours.

New Zealander **Maurice Bennet** creates **works of art out of toast.**

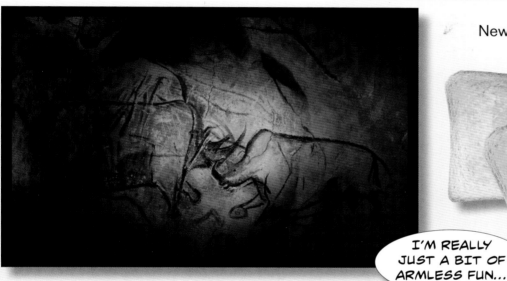

Where's the bear?

The **oldest paintings** in the world, at **Chauvet Cave** in **France**, show **lions**, **panthers**, **rhinos** and **bears** – all animals that **must have lived** in France when the paintings were done **35,000 years ago**.

I'M REALLY JUST A BIT OF ARMLESS FUN...

Chinese sculptor Zhu Cheng helped his art students create a **replica** of the famous Venus de Milo – **out of poo!**

I'M HAVING AN ICE TIME IN THIS HOTEL!

−273.15°C
(−459.67°F)

Absolutely freezing!

Did you know there is a **minimum temperature** where it **can't get any colder?** That temperature is **−273.15°C** (−459.67°F), or **0 kelvin (absolute zero)**. In 2003, scientists created the **coldest temperature ever** – only 0.0000000005°C above absolute zero.

Frosty reception for guests

Every winter in **Jukkasjärvi, Sweden**, thousands of people pay to **sleep on blocks of ice**. That's because they are staying at the **world's first** and **largest ice hotel**. The hotel is built **every winter** out of **blocks of ice** from the nearby Torne River – and then it **disappears** when summer comes and the **ice melts**. Guests **keep snug** by sleeping on **reindeer skins**.

Fantasy land

You might not **fancy taking a holiday** in a city where the temperature drops to **−30°C** (−22°F), the **wind howls** in from **Siberia**, and it **gets dark just after lunch**, but **a million people do** every year. They aren't in **Harbin, China**, for the weather, but to enjoy the **ice and snow festival** (pictured) – one of the **biggest** and **coolest ice festivals** in the world. There are hundreds of **buildings** and **sculptures made from ice** – some of them **bigger** than football fields. At night, **colourful lights** and **lasers** turn the festival into an **amazing wonderland**.

NOW EVERYBODY SAY 'FREEZE'...

Earning cold herd cash

The **Nenets** people of **Siberia** probably work in the **coldest conditions** in the world. They move **huge herds** of reindeer **thousands of kilometres** through the **Arctic Circle**. Temperatures often drop to **−50°C** (−58°F) as the Nenets and their animals cross **freezing plains** and **rivers**.

Super bug

If you **want** to live in a **really, really cold place**, you'd be best off being a **bacteria**. *Deinococcus radiodurans* is a bacteria that is **almost indestructible**. It survives extreme **cold**, extreme **heat** and extreme **radiation**!

COLDEST

Chill out in the coolest spots on Earth

Living in a freezer

Russia is the **biggest country** in the world, and also the **world's coldest country**. Its **average** temperature is **−5.5°C** (22.1°F), as most of the country is **much closer** to the **North Pole** than to the **Equator**. In some parts it is **so cold**, you could throw **boiling water** into the cold air, and it would **explode** into **vapour** and **ice**.

Sleeping with the fishes

A **funeral company** is building the world's **biggest underwater mausoleum**. The **Neptune Memorial Reef**, which opened in 2007 off the US state of **Florida**, will also be the world's **largest artificial reef** when it is finished. The **cemetery** will be a recreation of the mythical **Lost City of Atlantis**. There are already **plaques**, **columns**, **pathways**, **statues of lions**, and even **benches to sit on** in your wetsuit. They **mix people's ashes** into the concrete structures of the underwater city.

A frightfully ghoulish month

For **Chinese people**, the **deadest month** is their **seventh lunar month**. They call it **Ghost Month**. During this time, the **gates of Hell** are **flung open**, allowing the **souls of the dead** to **roam the Earth** and **pester** the living for **30 days** and **nights**. Many **temples** hold ceremonies where they **light lanterns**, **burn incense**, **offer food** to the ghosts and say prayers. During the **Hungry Ghost Festival**, people also put on **opera** and **puppet shows** to entertain the ghosts.

> I'LL KNOCK 'EM DEAD WITH MY KILLER OUTFIT

Big date with death

The **deadest day** on the **Mexican calendar** is the **Day of the Dead** on November 2. Funnily enough, the locals consider it a **happy day.** They visit the **graves of dead relatives** and bring them gifts, such as **flowers**, their **favourite food and drinks**, and even **toy or candy skulls** and **skeletons**. Some even have a **picnic** at the graves and a **sing-along**.

Seeing stars

The **deadest place** to get **buried** might well be **outer space.** At least it is **dead quiet** there! These days you can have your **ashes placed in a tube** the size of a lipstick case and have them **blasted into space** on a **rocket ship**.

DEADEST

Take a quick visit to the Other Side

This city is pretty dead

You have to be **dead keen** to visit the **'City of the Dead'**, near the remote village of **Dargavs** in **Russia**. These strange little houses are over **400 years old**. So are some of their **'residents'**, who holed themselves up inside and **died** of a **dreadful disease** called the **plague**. You can still see **skulls**, **bones** and **half-mummified bodies** in the houses, which are actually stone family burial crypts. Local **legend** still says that **anyone** who visits here **dies**.

Turning them in their graves

Every **seven years**, the **Malagasy** people in Madagascar **dig up dead relatives** and hold a **big** celebration. During the **'Turning of the Bones'** ceremony (Famadihana) they **wrap** the dead people up in **fresh silk cloth** and **dance with their bodies** around the tomb. Then they **return the bodies** to their graves.

INDEX

NOT-FOR-PARENTS EXTREME PLANET
Exploring the most extreme stuff on Earth!

1st Edition
Published September 2012

Conceived by Weldon Owen in partnership with Lonely Planet
Produced by Weldon Owen Publishing
Northburgh House, 10 Northburgh Street
London EC1V 0AT, UK

weldonowenpublishing.com

Copyright © 2012 Weldon Owen Publishing

WELDON OWEN LTD
Managing Director Sarah Odedina
Publisher Corinne Roberts
Creative Director Sue Burk
Sales Director Laurence Richard
Sales Manager, North America Ellen Towell
Concept Designer Hugh Ford
Designer Jacqueline Richards
Design Assistant Haylee Bruce
Index Puddingburn Publishing Services
Production Director Dominic Saraceno
Prepress Controller Tristan Hanks

10 9 8 7 6 5 4 3 2 1

Published by
Lonely Planet Publications Pty Ltd ABN 36 005 607 983
90 Maribyrnong St, Footscray, Victoria 3011, Australia

ISBN 978-1-74321-410-7

Printed and bound in China by 1010 Printing Int Ltd

A WELDON OWEN PRODUCTION

CREDITS

Key tl=top left; tcl=top center left; tc=top center; tcr=top center right; tr=top right; cl=center left; c=center; cr=center right; bl=bottom left; bcl=bottom center left; bc=bottom center; bcr=bottom center right; br=bottom right; bg = background

Front Cover Corbis bl, c, tcl; Getty Images bc, br; iStockphoto.com cr, tc; Nature Picture Library bcl

Back Cover Corbis bl, cl, cl, tc, tr; Getty Images bc; Nature Picture Library cr; Shutterstock tl

Spine Corbis c; Getty Images b

Alamy 65cr, 112tcr, tl, 131tc, 134cl, 149cl, 164-165bg, 176-177bc

Corbis 1tcl, 4bl, br, c, tr, 6br, tr, 11tr, 12-13bg, 16cl, 19tr, 22c, 22-23bg, 24bl, 29bc, 36-37bg, 39cr, 44cr, 45cl, 46tl, 46-47bg, 52-53bg, 55tr, 60bg, 60-61c, 63cl, 64-65bg, 67cl, 70cr, 71bcl, tcl, 72cr, 74-75bg, 75br, 76cl, 78-79bg, 80bl, 81tc, tcr, 82bc, bcl, bcr, bl, br, tr, 84bcr, tcr, 85tl, 86-87bg, 89bl, tl, 91c, tl, 94tl, 95br, 96bl, tc, 97bc, bl, br, tl, 98br, 104tr, 104-105bg, 105tl, 108bl, tl, 112bcr, 113tl, 114-115bg, 115bl, tr, 118-119bcs, 119br, 121cl, 124bcl, br, tl, 125tr, 128br, tc, 129br, tr, 130bc, cl, 131bl, br, 132-133bg, 133tr, 134cl, 136-137bg, 138cl, tl, 139br, cl, tcr, tl, 140bl, tr, 140-141bg, 141r, 143bl, 145tcl, 146bl, 146-147bg, 147tl, 148-149bg, 149tr, 150tl, 152-153bg, 153r, 156bl, tcl, tr, 157bl, cl, 159tr, 162tl, 165br, tl, tr, 166bl, 167tl, 170bl, 171bl, br, tr, 172cr, tl, 173br, cl, 174-175bg, 175br, tcl, 179bcr, tcr, 180bl, 180-181bg, 182bl, 183br, tr, 184tl, 184-185bg, 185tcl, tr, 186bl, tl, 187br, 190bl, 191br

Getty Images 4tl, 5br, 6bc, 7tl, 8bl, tl, tr, 13br, 16bc, tr, 16-17bg, 17bl, 18bc, 21tl, 31tr, 38tl, 38-39bg, 43bl, 46bl, 52tl, 53c, 54tl, 57tl, 62cr, 66-67bg, 71br, cr, tc, 73bc, cl, 77br, 78cl, 80-81bg, 81bcr, cl, 82tcl, 83br, tl, 84-85bg, 87bl, cl, tr, 92-93bg, 94br, 96cr, 100-101bg, 101tr, 102bl, tr, 103cr, 104tl, 108bl, cr, tc, 108-109bg, 109bc, 110-111bc, 112bl, tc, 112-113bg, 113br, 115bc, bcr, br, 116bl, tl, 117tl, 119cl, 120bl, 120-121bg, 121tr, tr, 122cl, cr, tr, 123c, tr, 125cl, 134br, br, tr, 136cr, tr, 137br, 140cr, 141tl, 142tr, 147tcr, 150cr, 152cr, cr, 152-153bl, 153bl, 156bcr, 157tr, 158bl, tl, 159br, cr, 162br, 163bcl, l, 166cr, 166-167bg, 167br, 169br, 172bc, 173tr, 174tl, 175bcl, tr, 176cl, tr, 177tr, 178bcr, 179tcl, 181bc, tr, 182cr, tcl, 186cr, 188tc, 189br

iStockphoto.com 6-7bg, 10br, 10-11bg, 14-15c, 15br, 20br, c, 21tr, 26bl, bl, 26-27bg, 27cr, tc, 30cl, 30-31bg, 32-33bg, 33tr, 34-35bg, 37c, cl, 40c, 40-41bg, 44bl, 44-45bg, bg, 45cr, 48tl, 51tl, 54-55bg, 56tr, 56-57bg, 57br, 58-59bg, 61bg, 62tcl, 66bl, cr, tl, 67c, tr, 72-73bg, 74bc, 76-77bg, 88-89bg, 93br, 95tcl, 100bl, 108cl, 108-109bg, 109tr, 110tc, tr, 118-119bg, 122-123bg, 134-135bg, 138cr, 144bl, 145br, 154bcl, 154-155bc, bg, tc, 158-159bg, 160tcr, 160tl, 188cr, 191tl

Bryan Lessard/CSIRO 76c

Sarah McLean 130tr

Nature Picture Library 2-3c, 17tr, 31bc, 34br, cr, 35tl, 43cr, 49tl, 50-51bg, 90bl, 103bcl, bcr, bl, br, cl, tcl, tcr, tl, tr, 134tc, 143cr, 147br, 148cl, tr, 149br, 150bl, 152bl, cl, 171cr, 179tcl, 185bl

Public Domain 98tcr, 138-139bg, 178-179bg

Shutterstock 1bc, c, 6bl, 7tr, 8br, 11bcr, cr, tcr, 13cr, tl, 16cr, 20bl, 20-21bg, 23br, 24cr, tl, 24-25bg, 25br, tcr, 27br, 28br, cl, 28-29bg, 32tl, 37tr, 38br, 39tcl, 40bl, br, tcr, 42cr, tr, 42-43bg, 43tl, 45tr, 46tcr, 47bc, 48br, 48-49bg, 50bl, cl, 51tr, 53tl, 54bc, bl, 62bl, 62-63bg, 63br, 69bl, 70-71bg, 77cl, 79tl, 84tl, 88cr, tl, 91bcr, 92tl, 96-97bg, 104bc, 105tl, 111tl, 114tl, 116cr, 117br, 124-125bg, 126-127bg, 130-131bg, 136bl, 142tl, cr, 143tc, tr, 145bl, 154tcl, 156bcr, bl, tcl, tr, 156-157bg, 157bl, cl, tr, 160bl, 161tl, 168bc, cl, 168-169bg, 169bl, 172-173bg, 178bl, cl, cr, 179bl, br, tl, tr, 181br, 182-183bc, 183cr, 186-187bg

SeaPics 23tl, 162cl, 163tl

Science Photo Library 27cl, 183cl

Topfoto 12tl, 95tr, 187cl

Gerard Vandystadt/Tips/Visualphotos 59tr

Wikipedia 16tl, 62tl, 76tr, 98cl, tl, 109cr, 115bcl, 171c

ILLUSTRATIONS

All illustrations by **Hugh Ford** except 46bcr **Peter Bull Art Studio;** 68c **James Gulliver Hancock/The Jacky Winter Group;** 111cr **Christer Eriksson**

All illustrations and maps copyright 2012 Weldon Owen Publishing

Also available in the series

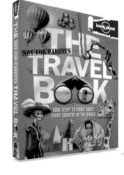

Country series books

City series books

LONELY PLANET OFFICES

Australia Head Office
Locked Bag 1, Footscray, Victoria 3011
phone 03 8379 8000
fax 03 8379 8111

USA
150 Linden St, Oakland, CA 94607
phone 510 250 6400,
toll free 800 275 8555
fax 510 893 8572

UK
Media Centre, 201 Wood Lane,
London W12 7TQ
phone 020 8433 1333
fax 020 8702 0112